Managing Workplace Stress

Koushiki Choudhury

Managing Workplace Stress

The Cognitive Behavioural Way

Springer

Koushiki Choudhury
Department of Marketing
Indian Institute of Management Calcutta
Kolkata, India

ISBN 978-81-322-0682-8 ISBN 978-81-322-0683-5 (eBook)
DOI 10.1007/978-81-322-0683-5
Springer India Heidelberg New York Dordrecht London

Library of Congress Control Number: 2012946641

Printed on acid-free paper

Springer is part of Springer Science+Business Media (www.springer.com)

Dedicated to
My Mother
For her love, inspiration and support

Preface

This book is offered with the hope that it will shed light on the many anxiety- and stress-inducing events that we face in the workplace and the ways to cope with them. The book is based on my experience, studies and research in the areas of internal marketing, psychological counselling and workplace stress and is the fallout of years of surveys and thousands of hours of talking to professionals in industry and academia, in the country and abroad. I have included snapshots of actual anxiety-producing situations that we all face in the workplace.

The book's objective is to enable people to change the way they view any unpleasant, disturbing and stressful situation and emerge more calm, confident and happy. It is offered with the understanding that even one entire lifetime is not enough to learn everything about such an extremely challenging area. I hence rely on the feedback from my readers to enable me to expand the frontiers.

I would like to thank my parents for their unfailing support at all times. To my father, for encouraging me to write and for always being there at the crucial moments with the right words. To my mother, who is my greatest source of inspiration and hope and to whom I owe everything.

Introduction

This is a self-help book that has been written for all those who are working and those who are about to enter the workplace. Workplace is defined as "any environment enabling work to be done". This broader definition will make the workplace include any situation and place where people interact to exchange knowledge, services and information.

The book discusses the various anxiety- and stress-inducing events that we face in the workplace and the ways to overcome them. The book is based on my extensive experience, research and studies in the areas of internal marketing, workplace stress and psychological counselling. I have included real-life scenarios of actual stress-, tension- and anxiety-generating situations that we all face in the workplace and have delineated the ways to address and resolve them using cognitive therapy (CT) and rational emotive behaviour therapy (REBT). These therapeutic techniques are the most widely used and powerful psychotherapeutic techniques, and their effectiveness has been thoroughly tested scientifically throughout the world. Briefly, cognitive behavioural therapy (also referred to as CBT – the umbrella term for CT and REBT together), which deals with identifying irrational negative thinking and replacing it with rational, realistic and healthier thinking, has been found to be effective for a wide range of emotional problems including anxiety and depression. The advantage of using psychotherapeutic techniques in addressing workplace stress is that it makes the approach scientific and therefore more reliable, robust, rational and effective. The book discusses the concepts of REBT and CT and attempts to show how these techniques can be used to challenge and overcome workplace stress by realistically and accurately interpreting events at the workplace. It also discusses irrational thinking and rational thinking, demanding rules and dogmas and the various techniques used in cognitive behavioural therapy (CBT). It sheds light on the multifarious cognitive errors that we suffer from, which results in faulty perception and interpretation of situations, thus enhancing anxiety. The objective is to achieve cognitive restructuring and move away from negative, distorted cognitive (thought) processes and towards more positive, realistic and rational thoughts. Hopefully, reading and practising these cognitive behavioural therapeutic techniques will enable the readers to overcome stress and anxiety at the workplace, emerge more attuned to reality and more calm, confident and happy.

Contents

1 **Workplace Stress** 1
So, Let Us Have a Quick Glance at the Major Factors That Have a Bearing on Stress at the Workplace 2
Fallout of Workplace Stress 4

2 **Rational and Irrational Beliefs** 7
Definition of Rational Emotive Behaviour Therapy 7
So, What Is Rational Thinking? 8
And What Is Irrational Thinking? 8
The Origin of Irrational Thinking 8
The Silver Lining 8
Irrational Core Beliefs (The Irrational MUSTs) 8
Acceptance 9
Unconditional Self-Acceptance 10
Unconditional Other-Acceptance 10
Unconditional Life-Acceptance (Leads to High Frustration Tolerance) 11
Disputing Our Irrational Beliefs 11

3 **The ABC Framework of REBT** 13
Situation 14
Disputing 16

4 **Cognitive Therapy (CT)** 19
Cognitive Therapy (CT) 19
Cognitive Errors 20
Example 1: Situation: Worked Hard – Yet Didn't Perform Well 23
Example 2: Incompetent Subordinate 24
Challenging My Cognitive Distortions 24

Negative Automatic Thoughts (NATs) and Dysfunctional Beliefs 25
Negative Automatic Thoughts (NATs) 25
Dysfunctional Beliefs 26
Recognizing Our Dysfunctional Beliefs 27
Example 28
Recapitulation of CT and REBT 34

5 Cognitive Behavioural Therapy (CBT) in the Workplace 37
How Can Cognitive Behavioural Therapy Techniques (CBT) Help Us in the Workplace? 37
Trying Situations Which We Face in the Workplace and Which Make Our Stress Go Through the Roof 37
Situation 1: Facing Criticism 37
Situation 2: The Abusive Boss 39
Situation 3: Carelessness 41
Situation 4: Conflicting Values 42
Situation 5: No Friends in the Office 43
Situation 6: My Views Not Being Recognized 45
Situation 7: People Going Back on Their Words 46
Situation 8: Saying Something Foolish 48
Situation 9: No Promotion Yet Again 49
Situation 10: Failing To Be Assertive 50
Situation 11: Being Alone Is Disheartening 52
Situation 12: Looking Back with Deep Regrets 54
Situation 13: Conflict with Friend 55
Situation 14: Others Taking Me for Granted 57
Situation 15: Not Keeping My Cool 58
Situation 16: Just Too Much Work 60
Situation 17: An Absolutely Vague Job 61
Situation 18: An Absolutely Boring Job 63
Situation 19: Disobedient Subordinates 64
Situation 20: No End to Seeking Approval 66
Situation 21: Can't Find the Ideal Solution 67
Situation 22: Failed to Meet My Targets 68
Situation 23: I Always Procrastinate 69
Situation 24: I Am Always Indecisive 70
The Advantages of Cognitive Behavioural Therapy (CBT) in the Workplace 71
Cognitive Behavioural Therapy (CBT) for Us 72

6 Conclusion 75

7 Exercises: Identifying and Challenging Distorted Negative Thoughts 79
Exercise 1: Lost Your Job 79
Distortions 79
Exercise 2: Failed in Your Job Interview 80
Distortions 81
Exercise 3: Not the All-Rounder 82
Distortions 82
Exercise 4: Feeling Inferior 83
Distortions 83
Exercise 5: Mundane Work 84
Distortions 85
Exercise 6: Being Laughed At 86
Distortions 86
Exercise 7: The Boss Is Dumping His Work on You 87
Distortions 87
Exercise 8: Feel Incompetent 88
Distortions 89
Exercise 9: Can't Stand Up for Yourself 90
Distortions 90
Exercise 10: Boss Does Not Like You 91
Distortions 91
Exercise 11: Failed to Do What You Had Planned 92
Distortions 92
Exercise 12: Lack Common Sense 93
Distortions 94
Exercise 13: You Help Others but They Don't Help You 95
Distortions 95
Exercise 14: Feeling Inferior 96
Distortions 96
Exercise 15: Never Speak Up at Meetings 98
Distortions 98
Exercise 16: Never Speak Up at Meetings (This Time for a Different Reason) 99
Distortions 99
Exercise 17: Never Speak Up at Meetings (For Yet Another Reason) 100
Distortions 100
Exercise 18: Complaint Against You 101
Distortions 101
Exercise 19: Impress the Chairman 102
Distortions 103

Exercise 20: A Disastrous Day 104
Distortions 104
Exercise 21: Interview After-Effects 105
Distortions 105
Exercise 22: Anxiety Jitters at Presentations 106
Distortions 107
Exercise 23: Not Popular 108
Distortions 108
Exercise 24: Ethical Dilemma 109
Distortions 110

References 111

About the Author 113

Index 115

Chapter 1
Workplace Stress

We are all acquainted with stress. We experience it in varying kinds every day. We experience it in varying degrees every day. We feel stressed when the demands we confront appear to exceed our capabilities to cope with them.

One of the major sources of anxiety and stress is our work. However, finding a low-stress job is not easy. In fact, it may be almost impossible. A more practical and sensible choice therefore would be to adopt effective strategies to cope with stress at work and reduce anxiety. Dealing with office politics; the hateful boss; the possibility of not getting a promotion or, worse, someone else being (undeservingly) promoted; too much work to do in too little time; a lack of clarity regarding what exactly you are expected to do; and, ultimately, the fear of getting fired can trigger anxiety attacks in every employee. Added to this is of course the interpersonal stress (thanks to some of our often annoying superiors, peers and subordinates) that we face in the workplace.

Moreover, most people are in jobs that they do not love. If you enjoy what you do, you are among the very few lucky ones. There are of course many reasons for staying in a job that you don't particularly like. The proverbial "golden handcuff" – the salary, the status, the prestige, the benefits, the perks and the pension – all these can keep you tied down to a job regardless of the unhappiness and the stress. The alternative solution is to find a job you like or one that better matches your talents, aptitude, skills, abilities and interests – again, an almost impossible task – easier said than done. Many of us have no idea what kind of job would suit us, taking into account all the things we desire in our prospective dream job. Worse, we often don't have a clue as to how to go about finding out all this information about a new job, because actually there is no way. There is no way you can know in advance what kind of job in what kind of organization will make you happy, unless you actually start working and experiencing all the positive and negative sides of your new job and your new company. Last but not the least, there is the inertia, the pain and the effort of looking for another job.

K. Choudhury, *Managing Workplace Stress: The Cognitive Behavioural Way*,
DOI 10.1007/978-81-322-0683-5_1, © Springer India 2013

So, Let Us Have a Quick Glance at the Major Factors That Have a Bearing on Stress at the Workplace

A. *Stress Arising out of Environmental Turmoil*
Turbulent economic and competitive conditions have resulted in substantial organizational restructurings, takeovers and mergers. These have turned out to be major stressors for employees. The upshot is that you have to work longer and harder just to maintain the lifestyle and economic status you have enjoyed so far. In this state of affairs, work overload prevails with too much work to do and too few people to do it, thanks to wholesale, random and indiscriminate lay-offs and freeze in hiring. Unrealistic expectations of performance (often during corporate restructuring, but otherwise also) leading to excessive unreasonable pressure on the employee completes the stressful picture. What is more, increased workload coupled with extremely long working hours, all for the same pay, can leave employees physically and emotionally drained. Employees today are putting in more and more hours per week at the office, carrying work home on weekdays, spending weekends in office or taking work home for the weekends. Moreover, the exponential growth in technology has resulted in increased expectations in terms of efficiency, productivity and pace of work. Employees feel that there exists a constant pressure to learn new technologies and keep abreast with technological advances, thus compounding the stress. Furthermore, excessive travel and too much time away from the family may make matters worse. Work underload is yet another outcome of this sorry situation. In many organizations and many departments, employees often find themselves with not having enough meaningful work to do. Consequently, the fear of redundancy and lay-offs creeps in. With the spate of restructuring, reshuffling, mergers and acquisitions and the consequent lay-offs happening, those who survive the lay-offs are often anxious, tense and fearful that they would perhaps be the next to go. The intense mental agony that laid-off employees experience (nervous breakdowns, depression, intention to harm self and others… the list is endless) need not be dwelt upon. Again, not all employees look forward to enhanced job responsibilities which are a fall out of unbridled organizational restructuring. They do not feel happy about career advancements or increased pay if it means supervising the work of many people, managing several subordinates or simply doing more work. Besides, with variable pay becoming more and more popular, employees face another stressor in terms of uncertain, fluctuating incomes.

B. *Stress Arising out of Workplace Interpersonal Milieu*
Maladjustment to workplace norms and cultures and the attitudinal characteristics of the boss, co-workers and subordinates may lead to subtle (or overt) interpersonal conflicts with them. Office politics, nepotism and office gossip can turn out to be major stressors. In fact, one of the most important stressors in the workplace is the interpersonal conflict that happens at work – conflicts, misunderstandings and disagreements with colleagues, superiors and

subordinates. To tell the truth, workplace violence, personal harassment and bullying at the workplace are on the rise all over the world. Often employees' race, their age, sexual orientation and physical disabilities if any become grounds for torment and consequent mental anguish in the workplace. Above and beyond, the employee may be asked to do certain things which are at cross purposes with his own moral values and pose an ethical dilemma. Rampant are incidents of employees being coerced to window-dress accounts, inflate sales figures and increase customer satisfaction indexes so that the company's results look good in the short run.

C. *Stress Arising out of the Job Structure and Framework*
Some degree of fluid boundaries are expected to occur as firms attempt to swiftly respond to the rapidly changing environment, for instance, say in response to customers' needs or competitors' moves. However, what employees face are persistent vagueness of job boundaries, lack of clarity about responsibilities, lack of clarity with regards to what exactly each employee is supposed to do, assignment of jobs in a haphazard manner and role ambiguity. These worsen the confusion of employees, especially when they are new to the organization. The problems get more pronounced when the firm is acquired by another one or merged into another one. An additional source of job stress is role conflict. An employee working at a bank experiences role conflict when her superior tells her to provide prompt, fast service to the customers (so that the queue in front of her does not get too long) and at the same time he tells her to persuade her customers to purchase the bank's financial products. Role conflict may also arise due to employees reporting to multiple bosses. Furthermore, often employees find themselves doing work which they do not consider as meaningful, where there is no variety and where their skills, interests and aptitudes are not matched with the work they are doing. All this happens due to a lack of proper thinking through and planning when it comes to job designing, hiring, training and motivational practices. Likewise, policies about job autonomy (e.g. allowing employees to make their own decisions about their jobs or about certain modules of their jobs) and employees' participation in company decisions are formulated arbitrarily without considering whether the right processes exist and whether the employees' temperaments, experience and skills are suited to such things. Last but not the least, a lack of proper career planning and career development opportunities, lack of promotional opportunities, subjectivity and arbitrariness in terms of promotion criteria, organizational politics, prejudices, biases and favouritism play havoc with career goals, thereby adding to the inventory of stressors.

D. *Stress Arising out of Work-Life Imbalance*
Each employee has different roles to play in life – he or she may be a parent with children to look after, a partner to someone who is perhaps pursuing a career and a son or daughter taking care of aged, sick parents. In such scenarios, threshing out a work-life balance equation can be extremely taxing and stressful.

E. *Stress Arising out of the Job Ambiance*

These include stressors arising out of unpleasant office ambiance, uncomfortable working conditions, unhygienic working conditions, poorly designed office spaces, lack of proper ventilation and improper temperatures, lighting and noise levels. Working in unsafe areas say such as in the mines and high-risk neighbourhoods in the cities, as well as working with radiation, dangerous diseases and hazardous chemicals, amplifies the stress that employees encounter. In the race, greed and voracity for more and more wealth and subsequent pressure for more cost savings, the strategies of many corporations seem to be profits at the cost of anything, regardless of employees' physical and mental well-being.

F. *Women and Workplace Stress*
Sexual harassment in the workplace is rife and has always been a major source of tension and worry for women. Moreover, women may suffer from stressors such as a hostile work environment, which is said to exist when an employee feels scared, uneasy, edgy or tense going to work because of the abusive, intimidating, threatening or oppressive atmosphere generated either by the boss, colleagues, subordinates or any other harasser. Last but not the least, subtle (or overt) discriminations at the workplace (the proverbial glass ceiling), gender biases, sexist attitudes, family pressures and societal obligations and demands add to the stressors.

Fallout of Workplace Stress

It is well known that at very low levels, job stress can stimulate performance and hence the saying "I work better under pressure". However, this is only true for very and I mean very low levels of stress. Anything more than these low levels of stress usually has disastrous effects on a person's physical and mental health and hence negatively affects an individual's performance.

The results of workplace stress vary from person to person, depending on the particular situation, how prone the person is to stress, how long the individual has been subjected to the stressors and the intensity of the stress itself. In fact, each of us reacts to stress differently. Each of us has a different level of anxiety and worry that we can handle without breaking down, and only we can assess our level of tolerance to stressful situations. One solution to stress is of course to avoid getting into situations that are likely to overwhelm our stress coping abilities. However, this is not always possible because there are certain situations which are extremely difficult to avoid or even unavoidable.

Typical initial symptoms of job stress could be:

- Anxiety
- Nervousness
- Distraction – lack of concentration
- Worry
- Frustration

- Irritability
- Anger
- Loss of motivation
- Absenteeism
- Insomnia
- Headaches

As the stress level intensifies, or if it becomes prolonged, a person may begin to feel more severe effects, such as:

- Depression
- Tremors and palpitations
- Panic attacks
- Physical problems such as heart disease, intense prolonged headaches, migraine, dizziness, gastrointestinal problems and neurological problems
- Substance abuse
- Conflicts and unhappiness in the family
- Intentions to harm others
- Intentions to harm self

What if we now look at the situation from the organization's point of view? Companies today are going all out in hiring consultants and experimenting with office ambiance, such as décor, colour, light, flooring, carpeting and the works, in their efforts to create optimal working conditions for employees. Aesthetically pleasing cafeterias and lounges are being added to the mix, with gyms and day care centres thrown in. Yet the problems of low employee morale, low productivity, absenteeism and high turnover remain. Why? Simply because employees are unhappy at the workplace. Simply due to workplace stress.

The focus of this book is to cope with workplace stress using psychotherapeutic techniques, namely, cognitive therapy (CT) and rational emotive behaviour therapy (REBT), together referred to as cognitive behavioural therapy (CBT). Both these psychotherapeutic techniques are based on the premise that when we become upset and unhappy, it is not the events taking place in our lives that upset us; it is the beliefs that we hold about these events that cause us to become depressed, anxious, worried, angry and miserable. The idea that our beliefs upset us has been around from times immemorial, arrived at by many thinkers. The Greek Stoic philosopher Epictetus observed around 2,000 years ago that "people are disturbed not by things or situations, but only by the views which they take of them".

Chapter 2
Rational and Irrational Beliefs

Definition of Rational Emotive Behaviour Therapy

Rational emotive behaviour therapy or REBT (Ellis 2001, 2007; Ellis and Harper 1997) as it is popularly known as was developed in the 1950s by the American psychotherapist Dr. Albert Ellis.

The cardinal concept of REBT is that events alone and by themselves do not cause a person to feel depressed, sorrowful, frightened, furious or highly anxious. Rather, it is one's beliefs and thoughts about the events which primarily cause unhealthy distressful feelings and self-defeating behaviours (behaviours that prevent us from being happy and/or are harmful for us). In other words, our emotional sufferings, miseries and sorrows result primarily, though not completely, from our perceptions and evaluations of a negative event and not solely by the event per se.

REBT states that humans have both rational and irrational tendencies – that is, humans tend to think both rationally and irrationally.

So, What Is Rational Thinking?

Rational thinking includes logically, realistically and pragmatically evaluating ourselves, others, the world and life as they really are. Rational thoughts lead to goal accomplishment; reduce conflicts with others; reduce frustrations, anxiety, guilt, anger and sadness; and bring mental peace and happiness. Rational thoughts are sensible, flexible and not self-defeating. They allow us to live harmoniously with reality.

K. Choudhury, *Managing Workplace Stress: The Cognitive Behavioural Way*, DOI 10.1007/978-81-322-0683-5_2, © Springer India 2013

And What Is Irrational Thinking?

Irrational thinking distorts and misinterprets reality in a way that causes emotional pain and distress – it is rigid, extreme, illogical, inflexible and mismatched with reality. It leads to poor emotional health.

According to REBT, irrational patterns of thinking and perceiving are the cause of much human disturbances, including depression, anger, guilt, frustration and anxiety. Irrational thoughts prevent goal achievement, lead to inner conflict and turmoil, lead to more conflict with others, low frustration tolerance, low self-esteem, jealousy and guilt. In short, irrational thoughts lead to emotional pain and suffering.

The Origin of Irrational Thinking

From where do our self-destructive irrational beliefs originate? Human beings begin life with an innate genetic predisposition to irrational thinking, which they then nourish by learning new, erroneous, unrealistic and often harmful ways of thinking, behaving and observing life. REBT teaches that though we learn some of the irrational beliefs during our childhood and pick up some from our environment as we grow up socially, human beings have strong inborn, natural biological tendencies to think irrationally and that these irrational beliefs grow stronger as a person continually revisits them.

The Silver Lining

The good news is that there is a positive side to human nature. Even though we are predisposed to often think irrationally, we also have the ability to think about and scrutinize our beliefs, analyse them and change the dysfunctional ones. Just as humans have strong innate tendencies to learn, whatever humans have learned, they can also unlearn and modify. REBT is a learning process which teaches us how to identify self-defeating thoughts and beliefs which are irrational, unrealistic, demanding, illogical and absolutist. It also teaches us how to mentally dispute these beliefs and replace them with more rational and self-helping ones. In fact, one of the main objectives in REBT is to show us that whenever unfortunate, unpleasant and adverse events occur in our lives, we have a choice of making ourselves feel healthily sorry, disappointed, frustrated and annoyed, instead of making ourselves feel unhealthily horrified, terrified, panicked and depressed.

Irrational Core Beliefs (The Irrational MUSTs)

Although we are all different people and communicate differently, the thoughts and beliefs that make us upset are all variations of some common irrational beliefs containing a rigid demand(s), either about ourselves, others, the world or life in general. These beliefs are (Ellis 2001, 2007; Ellis and Harper 1997):

- I MUST always be an excellent and competent performer. I MUST be likeable and endearing at all times. Otherwise, I am incompetent and worthless. I absolutely MUST impress others (or someone particular) with my social skills, my charm, my wit and my communication skills and win their approval, or else I am no good. Similarly, when having a conversation with someone I am trying to make an impression on, I MUST not run out of intelligent things to say and stop dead in mid-track. I MUST do well and be successful; otherwise, it will be TERRIBLE. I absolutely MUST not fail at work (instead of I prefer not failing at work – I don't like it). It will be AWFUL and HORRIBLE if I fail, and I will appear as worthless. I WILL NOT BE ABLE TO STAND my failure. These beliefs usually lead to feelings of worthlessness, depression, anxiety, panic, shame, despair and guilt.
- All important and significant people in my life MUST treat me considerately, courteously, kindly and fairly at all times (instead of I dislike being treated unfairly by others or taken advantage of) just as I would wish them to, or else I CAN'T STAND IT. If people don't treat me nicely, they are evil and SHOULD be severely punished and blamed for their hideous treatment of me. This kind of thinking leads to feelings of vengefulness, rage and inclination towards violence. Similarly, other people MUST not thwart my goals in life and MUST not block my progress in any way.
- Things and conditions absolutely MUST be the way I want them to be and MUST never be too difficult or frustrating. Conditions at my workplace MUST not be too hard. Otherwise, life is AWFUL, TERRIBLE, HORRIBLE, CATASTROPHIC and UNBEARABLE, and I CAN'T STAND IT. Similarly, it will be TERRIBLE and AWFUL if I lose my job (in place of it will be problematic, inconvenient, to my disadvantage and troublesome if I lose my job). In other words, I MUST get whatever I want and whenever I want it, and I MUST not get what I don't want. It's AWFUL, TERRIBLE and HORRIBLE if I don't get what I want, and I WON'T BE ABLE TO STAND IT. These kinds of beliefs lead to low frustration tolerance, self-pity, anger, depression and to behaviours such as procrastination, avoidance and inaction.

REBT teaches us that our belief system, based on MUSTs, SHOULDs, OUGHT TOs, NEEDs and HAVE TOs, is likely to create unrealistic, inaccurate, crooked inferences and distortions in thinking. When people overuse absolutistic and rigid "SHOULDs", "MUSTs", "HAVE TOs" and "OUGHTS", they will very likely disturb themselves due to the demanding nature of these words and the associated beliefs. It is therefore better if these rigid, demanding, extreme, unrealistic and inflexible ways of thinking are replaced with more realistic, flexible and self-benefiting attitudes. REBT does not dispute that a person should have desires and goals – so long as they are just that – strong preferences and wishes rather than demands.

Acceptance

To be emotionally healthy and to reduce emotional pain, we MUST accept reality, even when reality is highly harsh, unpleasant, tragic and unfortunate. REBT emphasizes that we develop (1) unconditional self-acceptance, (2) unconditional other-acceptance and (3) unconditional life-acceptance. Each of these types of acceptance is based on the following beliefs (Ellis 2001, 2007; Ellis and Harper 1997):

Unconditional Self-Acceptance

1. I accept myself irrespective of whatever acts I do and whatever traits I possess or do not possess. My self-acceptance is totally unconditional. My self-acceptance and the right to be happy are not dependant on what I accomplish, what I achieve or whether I get others' approval. Achievements or success do not increase my worth or value; failures do not make me less worthy or less valuable. I may feel happier after accomplishing a desired goal, but this does not increase my worth or my value. It does not make me a better or worthier person. I am valuable and worthy because I am alive. I shall not attempt to globally rate my being or my self. Instead, I will only evaluate my feelings, thoughts and actions as good or bad depending on whether they help me to achieve or frustrate my individual and social goals.
2. I am not a perfect human being; I have my good points as well as my bad points. I have my strengths and I have my weaknesses. I will accept myself as an imperfect, fallible human who will make many mistakes throughout life.
3. Taking into account all my good points and my bad points, all my strengths and my weaknesses, I am no more worthy and no less worthy than any other human being.

Unconditional Other-Acceptance

1. I shall accept other people unconditionally, even though I may dislike their behaviour.
2. There is no reason why other people ABSOLUTELY MUST or SHOULD treat me considerately, kindly and fairly. I will not demand that other people HAVE TO be fair and that they MUST change their bad behaviour. I may avoid them if they continue with their bad behaviour, though. In fact, other people will treat me inconsiderately, unfairly and unkindly from time to time. They will sometimes be mean, rude, unhelpful, selfish, ungrateful and obnoxious towards me. This is because just like me, they are not perfect either. We all do deeds which are very good, good, neutral, bad and downright bad. We all do things that are unfair, cruel, selfish and rude at times. This is because we are not perfect in terms of anything, including our own behaviour towards others. Moreover, people often do not realize that they are behaving badly. In fact, they may even think that we deserve their bad behaviour and the way they are treating us – once again, because no human being is perfect.
3. The people who treat me unkindly, inconsiderately and unfairly are as worthy and valuable as any other human being – no more or no less.

Unconditional Life-Acceptance (Leads to High Frustration Tolerance)

1. I will accept that life is full of difficulties, misfortunes, grief, uncertainties and injustices. Life will often not work out the way that I'd like it to.
2. There is no reason why life SHOULD and MUST be the way I want it to.
3. I will not define the unfortunate and bad things in my life as TERRIBLE, AWFUL and HORRIBLE. These words imply that the situation is totally bad, 100% bad. No situation is 100 % bad. Everything, every situation can be worse. Things can always be worse. This attitude will help me to cope more effectively with the unfortunate activating events in my life, prevent me from making them worse than they really are and help me to achieve high frustration tolerance. I will also keep in mind that life would indeed be better if I solved all my problems well, but it's not TERRIBLE OR AWFUL if I don't. I can still stand it and have a happy life in spite of some of my important problems remaining unsolved.
4. I will try my best to change what can be changed about the painful situations in my life and accept, though not like, what I cannot change.

To summarize, REBT teaches that:

- Unconditional self-acceptance, other-acceptance and life-acceptance are essential to achieve emotional well-being and mental peace.
- People and the world are imperfect. All humans do both good and bad deeds, have both positive and negative traits and attributes and are far too complex to be given single overall ratings.
- People are valuable and worthy just as a result of being alive. Perception about human self-worth is largely conceptual, definitional and not empirically verifiable. There is no definition of self-worth. Nor is there any benchmark for self-worth.

Disputing Our Irrational Beliefs

The aim of REBT is to help us change our irrational beliefs into healthy, logical, realistic, flexible and rational beliefs. This is accomplished by challenging and disputing our irrational beliefs. For instance, disputation may ask questions like, "Why MUST or SHOULD I succeed?" "Why MUST or SHOULD I win someone's or others' approval?" "Where does it say that other people MUST or SHOULD behave with me kindly, fairly or in a just manner?" Similarly, "Why MUST not others treat me unfairly and unkindly?" "Because I want a particular thing, why MUST or SHOULD I have it?" "Why MUST I get justice?" When we endeavour to reply to the disputing questions, we see that there are no rationale or grounds why we absolutely MUST or SHOULD have success, victory, appreciation, approval, kindness, fairness, integrity, uprightness or anything else that we attach importance to.

In a nutshell, REBT contends that though we are predisposed to think irrationally, we can confront our tendency to think so and work hard at changing our irrational, rigid and unrealistic beliefs. The challenge lies in the fact that as human beings even if we tell ourselves that we are thinking irrationally, in the core of our being, we hold onto our irrational thoughts extremely strongly. Thus, we continue to feel upset. Moreover, we rarely manage to keep these irrational ways of thinking away permanently. They often creep back. Thus, questioning, challenging and disputing our irrational beliefs and changing our ways of thinking takes intense practice. It also requires strong persistence. With perseverance and practice, the holds these irrational thoughts have on us gradually weaken and wither, and they lose their power to disturb us.

Chapter 3
The ABC Framework of REBT

REBT relies on a straightforward, simple ABC format to illustrate how our thoughts and beliefs lead to our emotional and behavioural responses (Ellis 2001, 2007; Ellis and Harper 1997). At the heart of REBT is this ABC theory of thought and behaviour.

The A in this ABC model stands for an activating adverse event, for instance, some type of challenging life situation. A could include events or experiences that prevent us or thwart us from achieving our goals. The A could include situations such as interpersonal conflicts, unsatisfying work, financial problems, health problems and all the many things that we think are the sources of our unhappiness. B stands for beliefs (and thoughts), especially the irrational, self-defeating beliefs in response to A that are the actual causes of our unhappiness. C is for consequences, the neurotic symptoms and painful emotions such as worry, depression, frustration, anxiety, misery, panic, rage and the associated behaviours that come from our beliefs.

Although the activating experiences may have caused us real pain, it is our irrational thoughts and beliefs that make matters worse and even more painful. We must therefore dispute (D) the irrational thoughts and beliefs, in order to enjoy the healthy emotional effects of rational beliefs.

The ABC framework illustrated below helps to clarify the relationship between activating adverse events (A), our thoughts and beliefs about them (B) and the consequences of our beliefs (C). It also shows how the framework distinguishes between the effects of rational beliefs about unpleasant or unfortunate events, which give rise to healthy negative emotions, and the effects of irrational beliefs about unpleasant or unfortunate events, which lead to unhealthy negative emotions.

K. Choudhury, *Managing Workplace Stress: The Cognitive Behavioural Way*,
DOI 10.1007/978-81-322-0683-5_3,

A = The Adverse Activating Event
- What exactly happened?

B = Beliefs and Thoughts About the Adverse Activating Event
- What did you tell yourself about the event?
- What did you think about the event?

C = Consequences
- What were your feelings?
- How did you behave or act?

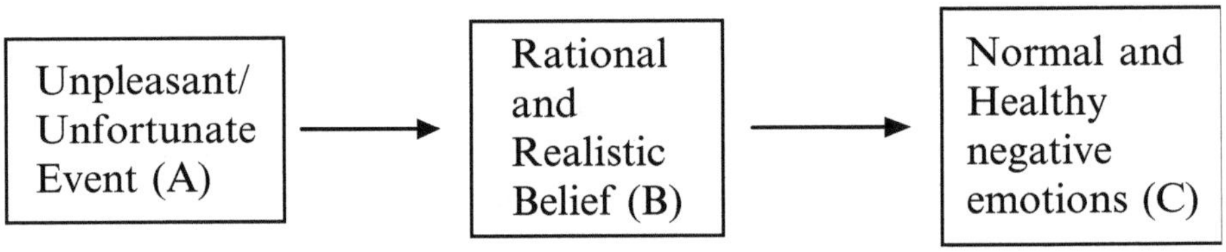

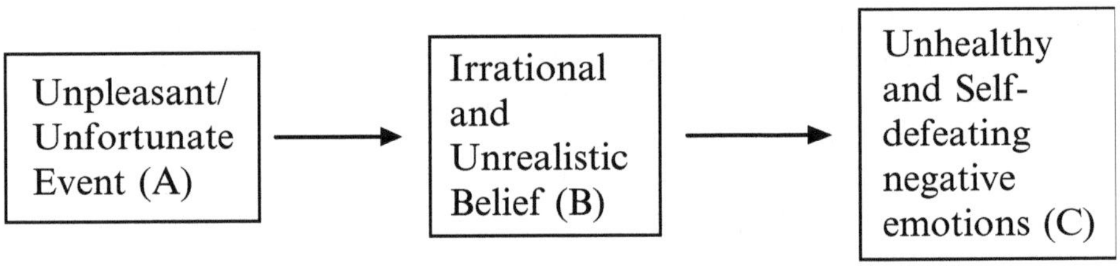

Thus:

A. An unpleasant or unfortunate event happens.
B. You have a thought or belief about the situation or event.
C. You have an emotional and behavioural reaction to your thought or belief.

So, let us go through an example of this ABC format.

Situation

One day, you met the president of your company, Mr. Roberts, at the office party. You greeted him but he did not return your greeting, to which you reacted negatively. Here is the adverse event, your beliefs and thoughts as well as your emotional reactions put in the ABC format:

A. *The Adverse Event: What Triggered Things*
Met the president, Mr. Roberts, at the office party. I greeted him but he did not return my greeting.

B. *Your Beliefs and Thoughts About A*
He ignored me.

C. *Your Reaction*
Feelings: Feeling inferior, inadequate
Behaviours: Since Mr. Roberts is in such a high position, it is obvious that he would ignore such a small fry like me. I am way too small, too unimportant and much too lowly for him. In future, I should lower my expectations in such situations.

Now, *someone who thought differently than you* about the same event would react in another way:

A. *The Adverse Event: What Triggered Things*
Met the president, Mr. Roberts, at the office party. I greeted him but he did not return my greeting.

B. *Your Beliefs and Thoughts About A*
Mr. Roberts MUST be terribly angry with me. I wonder whether I have ever made any disparaging comment about him to my colleagues and if Mr. Roberts has come to know about it. God knows what damage Mr. Roberts can do to my career. I have heard that he is kind of vindictive. That would be terrifying. The job market is really bad now.

C. *Your Reaction*
Feelings: Extreme anxiety
Behaviours: Oh dear! I can't recollect whether I had some time or the other criticized Mr. Roberts to my colleagues! Otherwise, why would he ignore me? Why can't I be smart instead of being so frank and open with people? What will I do if I lose my job? Or if I am transferred to a remote place?

Again, another person *who thought differently than you* about the same event would react in yet another way:

A. *The Adverse Event: What Triggered Things*
Met the president, Mr. Roberts, at the office party. I greeted him but he did not return my greeting.

B. *Your Beliefs and Thoughts About A*
May be he did not hear me. He might have been totally engrossed, thinking of something else.

C. *Your Reaction*
Feelings: Kind of neutral
Behaviours: Just to make sure, I will observe how he behaves the next time we pass each other or meet. No point in jumping to conclusions.

This example shows how *different ways of viewing the same event can lead to different reactions.*

Thus, the ABC example and framework shows that *A* (the adverse event) does not cause *C*. It is *B* (your thoughts and beliefs) that causes *C*. In the first example, it is not Mr. Roberts not returning your greeting that makes you feel inferior; it is your belief that he deliberately ignored you. In the second example, it is not Mr. Roberts not returning your greeting that makes you terribly anxious; it is the belief that he is very angry with you and therefore might jeopardize your career. In the third situation, the same event is actually not disturbing you and you are relatively calm.

Let us take a look at another example:

A. Your boss wrongly charges you of removing the confidential performance appraisal file from his desk.
B. You believe (think), "He has no right to falsely charge and implicate me. He's simply sinister!"
C. You feel incensed and furious.

If you thought differently, your emotional reaction would have been different:

A. Your boss wrongly charges you of removing the confidential performance appraisal file from his desk.
B. You believe (think), "I hope he does not tell the senior management and makes it an issue to fire me. I MUST not lose my job in any case – definitely not in such an undignified manner. I will not be able to stand it if I lose my job. That would be simply too much to take".
C. You feel anxious to the point of near panic.

Again, with this example, the ABC model shows that A (the adverse event – that is, what happens) does not cause C (your emotional reactions and feelings). It is B (your thoughts and beliefs) that leads to C. In the first case, it is not your boss's false allegation or indictment that makes you feel bitter and fly into a rage; it is your thought and your conviction that he is evil and has no right to incriminate you. In the second case, it is not your boss's allegation that makes you anxious, worried and panicky; it is your thought and your belief that, come what may, you MUST not lose your job and that losing your job would be the end of the world. It would be simply excruciating, unacceptable and unbearable for you.

Disputing

Up till now, we have discussed the ABC part of the REBT framework. Disputing is the *D* phase of the ABC model. To reiterate, disputation may ask questions resembling, "Why MUST or SHOULD I achieve a lot?" "Why MUST or SHOULD I be successful?" "Why do I NEED to be successful?" "Why MUST or SHOULD I win others' appreciation or love?" "Where is it written that other people MUST or SHOULD treat me with kindness, fairness and consideration?" "Because I desire something, why MUST or SHOULD I have it?" When we try to answer the disputing questions, we see that there is no reason why we absolutely MUST have success, approval, consideration, benevolence, thoughtfulness, justice, fair dealings, righteousness or anything else that is significant to us. As an illustration, let us consider the thought "I MUST have approval". We of course desire approval and acceptance and that is perfectly natural and healthy, because it enables us to perform well (we would prefer to win the approval of our bosses, colleagues, project team members, our subordinates, our professors, our students) and achieve our goals in our workplace, at home and in our lives in general. However, there is a difference between demanding approval and wanting (or preferring or desiring) approval. We definitely do not need approval to survive, though we may greatly desire it. There are differences between needs and wants. We may want a million things, but we definitely do not need most of those.

Chapter 4
Cognitive Therapy (CT)

Cognitive Therapy (CT)

According to cognitive therapy (CT), the way we think about events influences how we feel and behave. In other words, it's not the adverse event that makes us unhappy; it's how we think about and view the event that does it. It's one's opinions, thoughts and beliefs about unfortunate events that affect one's feelings, behaviour and subsequent actions. The hallmark of CT is that if thoughts and beliefs do not change, there is no improvement in one's mental condition. If thoughts and beliefs change, symptoms change. Dysfunctional feelings and behaviour are caused due to dysfunctional thinking. Hence, if we can change our thinking, we will change the way we feel and behave. After identifying and analysing inaccurate, negative, irrational and distorted thoughts, CT seeks to replace these thoughts with more rational, healthy and realistic ones. CT has been widely tested scientifically and found to be effective for many kinds of emotional problems including anxiety, depression, fears, anger management, addiction problems, personality disorders, phobias, obsessional disorders, somatization disorders, panic disorders and numerous severe psychiatric disorders as well.

One of the pioneers in CT is the psychiatrist Aaron Beck. Beck (1976) proposed that the negative thinking which is prevalent in depression originates in ideas, beliefs and assumptions which are laid down in childhood and built up with the years. For example, let's take the common assumption: "To be valuable and worthwhile I must be a high-achiever. I must be successful". This may be useful as far as motivating someone to perform better is concerned. However, in case the person fails at an important examination or evaluation, he might think that he is *worthless, a total disaster and an utter failure as a human*. This will lead to lowering his mood, which can lead to more negative and gloomy thoughts appearing, which in turn can lead to depression. Depression makes him resort to more negative, dark thinking about himself, his life, the world and his future. He starts feeling helpless, hopeless and worthless. Thus, a vicious cycle ensues.

K. Choudhury, *Managing Workplace Stress: The Cognitive Behavioural Way*,
DOI 10.1007/978-81-322-0683-5_4, © Springer India 2013

Cognitive Errors

Cognitive errors are distortions and inaccuracies in our thoughts that form the foundation of our painful feelings. Disturbed evaluations of situations often occur due to these cognitive errors. In fact, we frequently make cognitive errors, and the habit gets more pronounced during stressful situations. This results in faulty, illogical and unrealistic perception and interpretation of adverse situations and events. Consequently, the anxiety level increases. The objective of CT is to move away from negative, distorted cognitive (thought) processes and towards more positive, realistic and rational thoughts. So what are some of the cognitive errors that cause us so much unhappiness? These are (Burns 1999; Beck 1976; Beck et al. 2005):

Overgeneralization – When we overgeneralize, we conclude that the adverse thing which happened to us once or twice will happen again and again. Hence, we feel distressed. For instance, "This is my third job interview and I failed yet again… I am never going to get a job", says the person who overgeneralizes. Some other instances of overgeneralization are:

- One person at work does not like me and tells me so. I had always felt that he did not like me, but now he has said it in so many words. Hence, I know it is not my wrong judgement. I then assume that no one at work likes me. This is a typical example of the distorted thinking associated with overgeneralization.
- I try my hand at a new hobby and initially my performance does not turn out to my satisfaction. I therefore conclude "I'm just not good at things like this".

All-or-nothing thinking (also called *black-and-white thinking or dichotomous thinking*) – This is about viewing things (including our life experiences and personal traits) in extreme ways, in totally contrasting opposite categories, with no middle ground – excellent or terribly bad, success or failure, right or wrong, moral or immoral and so on. There is only black or white but nothing in between. The colour grey does not exist. For instance, "I did not get a promotion. So that means I am a loser – a total failure". This kind of thinking is totally unrealistic, because things, our traits and our life experiences are never totally black or white, one or zero. Nobody is absolutely honest or absolutely dishonest. Nobody is absolutely intelligent or absolutely foolish. This pattern of thinking is associated with perfectionism. This kind of thinking makes us afraid of any errors that we make or any imperfections in the situations we experience, because we then see ourselves as total failures and our experiences as totally dismal. We thus feel miserable, inadequate and worthless.

Mental filter (also called *selective abstraction*) – This includes selecting out and magnifying the negative element in a situation and focusing on it exclusively. Consequently, the entire situation appears to us shrouded in a gloomy, negative light. For example, "I got a C in Finance and that is terrible", says a student, failing to give due importance to the fact that he earned A's and B's in other subjects.

Labelling – This involves creating a completely derogatory self-sketch, based on our mistakes and failures. For example, I make an error and think: "I am a failure", instead of "I made an error". Labelling is irrational because human beings do so many things, good, bad and mediocre throughout their complicated lives, that they cannot be defined by any single thing they do. Similarly, when we label other people we evaluate their selves globally instead of evaluating their particular actions. This makes us more embittered towards them, and when we act on our feelings the other person retaliates, creating a vicious cycle of animosity.

Mind reading – This involves making guesses about what other people are thinking, and we are so convinced we are correct that we don't bother to check things out. Examples include "He ignored me on purpose" or "He's angry with me. That's why he did not talk to me". However, I really don't know for sure why he did not talk to me. Maybe he was brooding on the way the stock market and his wealth were steadily going down, and so he didn't notice me.

Fortune telling – Treating our feelings and beliefs about the future as though they would definitely turn out to be true and take place, rather than mere predictions. For example, "I'll be struggling financially for the rest of my life. There will be no end to my misery. Things can only get worse". The result of fortune telling is that we feel downright sad and hopeless. We forget that our feelings are based on our thoughts, and if these thoughts are inaccurate or distorted, our associated emotions will be invalid.

Emotional reasoning – Thinking that because we feel a certain way, this is how it really is in reality: "I feel I will never get well. This means that my disease is incurable. I will remain an invalid my entire life." "I feel drained and exhausted simply thinking about the huge pile of paperwork that has to be tackled. I know finishing it will be just impossible." This kind of thinking leads us to task avoidance and procrastination. We do not even attempt to start the work. Once we do start it, we see that the workload is not as frightening as we had perceived it to be. Once again, as in fortune telling, we forget that our feelings are based on our thoughts, and if these thoughts are inaccurate or distorted, our allied emotions will be unfounded.

Personalization – This refers to assuming ownership and responsibility for a negative event, even when there is no ground or reason for doing so. For example, "I MUST be a bad teacher; that is why my students did not do well". This, in spite of the fact that further investigation might reveal that the students did not study hard enough either. We conclude without any basis that the fault lies with us and is a reflection of our competence, knowledge, capabilities, etc. Personalization leads us to feel unreasonably guilty, as if we are responsible for everything negative that is happening. For instance, say I am a salesperson. As a salesperson, I can only influence my customer to buy my goods and services, but I cannot expect to control him. Ultimately, what the customer does, whether he buys, whether he does not buy or whether he defers the buying decision, is his choice as a thinking adult. It is his decision. Similarly, as an executive, an administrator or a teacher, I can only attempt to influence the people at my workplace, my subordinates or my students, as the case may be. I cannot control them or make them do a certain thing. What they chose to do is their own responsibility, their choice and not mine, as they are adults with the capability to think and decide.

Magnification [also known as *catastrophizing* (Ellis and Harper (1997)] – This occurs when a negative event, any mistake that we have made or any of our imperfections is blown totally out of proportion. For instance, "I made an error in the calculation of projected net profit. This disastrous event will ruin my image and reputation!" The original event is perhaps unpleasant, but the catastrophized event is "terrible, awful and unbearable". Catastrophization inflates and exaggerates ordinary negative events into extraordinary disasters and leads to frustration intolerance.

Minimization – The opposite of magnification, here we deflate our strengths, successes and other positive happenings in our lives. We of course tend to minimize others' weaknesses and their imperfections as well. Related to minimization is the *disqualifying the positive* bias, which occurs when people pay attention to positive information but then find a reason to not count it as they form their appraisals – that is, they have the amazing ability to misperceive good or neutral experiences as bad ones. "It is true that my boss praised my performance in the meeting today, but he only did that because he wanted to encourage me since I am new in the company."

If we magnify other people's strengths, their accomplishments and our imperfections and minimize other people's imperfections and our strengths, the end result will be that we will feel inferior and our self-esteem will take a beating. Moreover, we will not be able to appreciate the positive things that have happened in our lives.

So how do we achieve the cognitive restructuring that is the bedrock of CT? This is achieved by asking the following questions with regard to our negative, distorted thoughts about a particular event:

- What is the evidence supporting the view or thought currently held by us?
- What are the alternative explanations possible? – What is another alternative way of looking at the same event/situation but reaching another conclusion? Are alternative interpretations possible?
- What evidences would contradict our thoughts, viewpoints and opinions?
- Are we making cognitive errors? If so, which ones?
- If the current thought or belief is correct, what will happen in that case? What is the worst that can happen?
- Is the information we are relying on reliable?
- Are we confusing our feelings with facts?
- Are we thinking "this IS going to happen", rather than, "this MAY or COULD happen"? – Most of the time we worry about things that will never happen or arrive at the worst case scenarios without exploring and analysing all angles.
- Are we confusing high probability events with low probability events?

These questioning techniques aid in challenging distorted, irrational and inaccurate thoughts and help the stressed individuals benefit from greater clarity and understanding of their thinking processes. Faulty logic and erroneous beliefs and assumptions which lead to stress are attacked head-on, thus helping the individual cope with his emotional distress and ultimately overcome it. *Let us look at two examples*:

Example 1: Situation: Worked Hard – Yet Didn't Perform Well

Situation: I worked so hard – yet I didn't perform well in the evaluation. This is unthinkable. I can't bear it.

Erroneous assumption: If I am intelligent (or work hard), I will be successful.

What makes this idea irrational or maladaptive is the belief that it is always absolutely true and correct. Sure, working hard does increase our chance for success, but success is not guaranteed because the cause of success is multifactorial – meaning, that a lot of factors, including organizational politics, favouritism, the means and/or criteria of evaluation used, the subjectivity of the evaluation process, the mood of the evaluator at the time of evaluation and even the nature of the evaluator, contribute to success or failure. It is a fact that there are times when we do everything right, we make sincere efforts and yet we still don't get what we want. However, if we jump to the conclusion that we are incompetent or will never be able to make it because success has eluded us, the result will be a loss of self-esteem, unhappiness, unwillingness to make further efforts, loss of motivation and ultimately melancholy.

Some of the other-demanding or SHOULD rules that lead to frustration in the workplace include:

1. I SHOULD be able to find smooth and fast solutions to all my problems.
2. If I am polite and nice to my colleagues, they SHOULD be equally polite and nice to me. Well, not really – not always. Often maybe, if I am nice to them, they will be nice to me but not always. They will behave according to their own wishes, their own values and of course their own moods. In fact, how we behave with others is a function of our genes, how we have been brought up, our values and our life experiences so far. Hence, for people who generally behave badly with us, who are generally rude, insensitive, self-centred, manipulative and vindictive, expecting them to behave courteously, kindly, unselfishly and understandingly may not be very realistic.
3. Others SHOULD believe in and operate according to my standards, my value system and my ideas of what is good, moral and fair.
4. My subordinates SHOULD try to match my performance standards.

We must not forget that whatever (events, situations, interpersonal problems) causes us disappointment and grief do so because they do not meet our expectations. However, the unfortunate situations that we encounter in the workplace or otherwise, constitute reality – they are definitely the hard truth, because they are taking place. They are cold hard facts. This implies that our expectations are unrealistic in the first place. No wonder they make us miserable. We can attempt to shape, persuade, mould and influence people and processes (the reality, that is) and bring them closer to our expectations and desires. However, this may not always be feasible when other people are involved, because others' ways of thinking, their views, their self-interests, their constraints, their desires, their tastes, their values and beliefs of what is proper or improper, what is right or wrong, correct or incorrect will frequently be very different from ours. Hence often the easiest way to tackle unfortunate circumstances and situations is to lower or alter our expectations, and if possible compromise.

Example 2: Incompetent Subordinate

Example 2: I am extremely angry with my subordinate. I am not at all satisfied with his work. I expect and demand much better work from him. I am downright frustrated with his casual attitude and his sloppy work.

Challenging My Cognitive Distortions

Why my subordinate should perform better	Rational responses as to why my subordinate may not perform better
Our company has a culture of excellence. Each of us is expected to do a very good job	He (my subordinate) is probably thinking that he is doing a fairly adequate job vis-à-vis his pay
He should be more meticulous and careful about his work	Why should he be more careful and meticulous?
Because I would have been more meticulous in his place	But I am I and he is he – he is not me. He has his own value systems. He is working according to his standards, trying to meet his performance standards, not mine. His frame of reference and standards are obviously different from mine. Once again, he is probably thinking that he is performing fairly adequately vis-à-vis his pay
He should do an excellent job	Should he? Am I entitled to get whatever I desire just because I so desire? If not, then where is this "should" coming from? Moreover, are my expectations from him unrealistic? After all, not everyone does a good job. If we rate the performance of all our subordinates in our organization or in my own functional area and calculate the mean (average), 50% of the subordinates will be below the mean (average) in performance! That's why we have the concepts of mean (average) and median in the first place! So why have I such rigid, unrealistic expectations of good work from him? Not everyone will perform according to my ideals, standards and values! In fact, how can I expect that other people will measure up to and operate according to my standards? They will work according to their own standards! The word "excellent" is highly subjective. Each of us is a different person with different beliefs and ideas of what's good, mediocre and bad with regard to a job performance. So on what basis am I saying that he "should" do an excellent job? What's more, my subordinate is not deliberately performing badly to displease me. It's just that that's how he works. Besides, I have some subordinates reporting to me who are very good in their work. It is unrealistic and perfectionistic (hence unattainable) on my part to expect that all of my subordinates will be first-rate.

Take home point: I can calmly ask my subordinate to rectify his mistakes and not to repeat those mistakes (there's no guarantee that he won't repeat, since that is the way he works – in which case, I may have to point out his errors time and again). However, there's absolutely NO POINT in getting angry and worked up with him for his less than satisfactory (according to my standards) performance. In this case, anger is totally futile since it is ridiculous to expect that his mediocre capabilities "should" be better than what they are (after all, it depends on his genes to a large extent!). If I get angry with him, not only will it increase my inner agitation and turmoil, it will make him defensive (since no one likes to be controlled or forced to do anything), and he will retaliate. This would make me feel worse emotionally. In fact, I would feel miserable later thinking about how I lost my temper. I would ruminate about it for a long time. That would be really painful for me. In these kinds of situations, I will not benefit from my anger. It will not help me in any way. What I can try to do is appreciate my subordinates' strengths, his positives and complement him on these before I ask him to rectify his errors. Often it works. I may ask him if he is having any problems understanding or doing the work assigned to him and help him if required. I can try to find out if he likes what he is doing and whether he thinks it matches with his strengths and interests. If he thinks that his talents are more suited for some other type of work which he would enjoy more, I can discuss those options with him. Finally, even with my subordinates who are much better performers than this guy, if I expect and demand perfect, mistake-free work from them, I will make myself extremely disappointed, unhappy and agitated.

Negative Automatic Thoughts (NATs) and Dysfunctional Beliefs

The cognitive framework of emotional problems identifies two different classes of distorted thoughts. These are: Negative Automatic Thoughts and Dysfunctional Beliefs – Beck (1976), (Beck et al. 2005).

Negative Automatic Thoughts (NATs)

Negative automatic thoughts are unpleasant, distressing thoughts that are automatic and involuntary in nature. They are a creation of our cognitive errors. They are *negative* in the sense that they are irrational, distorted, thwart and frustrate motivation and contribute to emotional problems. They often make us feel gloomy, sad, morose, enraged and hopeless. In fact, these NATs may trigger the typical symptoms of anxiety such as a racing, palpitating heart and a feeling of nervousness, disquiet and unease. They are *automatic* in the sense that they seem to occur suddenly, very swiftly, just like that, appearing in the individual's head as if from thin air. In fact, unless the person specifically focuses his attention on what he is thinking, the NATs may pass unnoticed. All that the person would then be aware of is a sudden feeling of anxiety, discomfort and distress and maybe even a desire to escape the situation. For instance, someone may have the NAT while talking to a group of colleagues "they think I am a dull, boring person". This thought will be reinforced if while talking, he catches one of his colleagues checking his cell phone messages. Needless to say, our NATs are riddled with cognitive errors. Having identified our NATs, the next step is to find alternative, more realistic ways of thinking about the situation by examining the NATs for their rationality and robustness with regard to objective impartial evidence and accuracy.

Dysfunctional Beliefs

Dysfunctional beliefs are the deeply entrenched general views that we hold about ourselves, life, society, other people, humanity at large and the future. Formed during our early years, they make us prone to perceive and interpret adverse events and situations in a highly negative and dysfunctional manner. They serve as a filter for our life experiences and make us interpret certain situations in exceedingly rigid, extreme, exaggerated and threatening ways. These dysfunctional beliefs thus work against us, preventing us from finding serenity, happiness and hope. As a rule, they are unrealistic, distorted and highly inflexible. For illustration, a person who holds the dysfunctional belief that intrinsic human worth is linked with social approval (everyone must be fond of me, appreciate me and like me; otherwise, I am worthless) may perceive and interpret silent pauses in a conversation as a sign that others talking to him find him uninteresting, boring and maybe even peculiar. To all of us, however, our dysfunctional beliefs appear to make a lot of sense and seem pretty reasonable, since we have grown up with them. Often dysfunctional beliefs hibernate until activated by the appropriate situation. A beneficial, helpful and wholesome belief is one that lends itself to re-exploration in the light of alternative viewpoints and new evidences. Thus, it will be malleable and accordingly reconstructed by new realistic evidences, even if the latter are contrary to the previously held rigid, distorted beliefs. Dysfunctional beliefs on the other hand tend to be inflexible. For example, a deeply embedded belief "I am a bad person", even though I have done many good deeds in the past, is unrealistic and incorrect. It is dysfunctional. A more realistic, rational and healthy belief would be something like: "I may have behaved badly this time. However, this does not make me a bad person. Often I am patient, considerate, helpful and kind."

Dysfunctional beliefs which underlie depression and anxiety may be highly varied. Often, however, what makes us anxious and worried are dysfunctional beliefs revolving around issues like capability and competence, approval and acceptance, ownership and responsibility, power and control and anxiety symptoms (Beck et al. 2005). Examples would include the following:

Beliefs related to power and control – I have to be in control at all times, in all situations, always. My problems can only be solved by me.

Beliefs related to anxiety symptoms – It is terrible to appear anxious. I must always be cheerful and calm. We actually make ourselves anxious about our anxiety and depressed about our depression! No wonder it becomes a vicious cycle!
Beliefs related to approval and acceptance – I am useless and worthless unless I am appreciated and loved. I always need to make others happy and please them. If someone criticizes me, he is putting me down personally.
Beliefs related to ownership and responsibility – I am responsible for my subordinates' performance. I am responsible for my students' performance (we really don't know how hard the students worked – they may not have put in that much effort). I take ownership of these. I am largely accountable and responsible for others' happiness and enjoyment when they are with me.
Beliefs related to capability and competence – People are either victors or failures. There is no middle ground. Making mistakes implies that I am a failure. Unless a performance is perfect it is not acceptable.

Recognizing Our Dysfunctional Beliefs

As is often the case with any problem, recognition is the first step towards solution. Being alert to and simply recognizing what our dysfunctional beliefs and rules are and when they are operating is often enough to help us feel better. Any time we experience a negative emotion say like sorrow, anxiety, guilt, frustration or anger is a good indication that a dysfunctional belief may be at work. A good way to reveal our dysfunctional beliefs is to use the *Downward Arrow Technique (also known as the Vertical Arrow Technique)* (Burns 1999).

In the Downward Arrow Technique, we bring our worries and anxieties out into broad daylight and dissect them. We attempt to explore and identify the apprehensions, fears, discomfort and concerns that are serving as springboards for our anxieties and worries. We identify the distressing, unpleasant emotions and negative thoughts experienced within a problem situation. We then ask ourselves, "If this thought was true, right or accurate, what would happen then? What would that mean to us?" OR "What would be so bad about that?" OR "What would that say about us?" We operationalize the process by drawing a vertical downward arrow directly beneath our first automatic negative thought and asking ourselves "If this automatic thought were actually correct and true, what would happen in that case? What would it imply and mean to us? Why would it be distressing to us? What would be so dreadful about that?" Then we write down the next automatic thought that immediately comes to mind in response to the above questions. Every time we come up with a new automatic thought, we draw a downward vertical arrow beneath it and ask ourselves, "Even if this were true and the scenario actually happened, why would I feel upset? What would happen then?" As we do this exercise over and over with all our automatic thoughts, we will generate a linked series of thoughts that will reveal the core dysfunctional beliefs which are fuelling our emotional problems. Thus, the root causes of our stress, anxiety and misery get exposed, thereby enabling us to challenge them and consequently overcome them. It is also important to substitute a rational response that shows why our automatic thought is unrealistic, distorted, illogical and invalid. This helps us alter our ways of thinking; enables us to think about ourselves, our experiences and our lives in a more unbiased, objective, realistic and rational way; and consequently uplifts our mood and makes us feel calmer.

The strength and effectiveness of the Downward Arrow method lies in the fact that it is Socratic. Through a process of insightful questioning, we discover in a methodical, logical and unbiased manner the beliefs that make us miserable. We discover the source of our problems by repeating the following questions again and again: "If that negative thought were true (or correct), so what? What then? What would happen then? What would happen in that case? What would it imply or mean to us? Why would it distress and upset us? What would be the consequences?"

Example

As an illustration of this, let's take a salesperson named Neil. Neil is feeling absolutely terrible because he failed to clinch a certain big order. He is worried and anxious and feeling down throughout the day. We will embark upon the Downward Arrow journey by asking Neil to state one of his tormenting worries. Suppose Neil chooses the following:

> I'm worried that my boss will think that I am incompetent because I failed to get this lucrative order.

Now, this is a fairly regular, typical worry. Most of us often worry about such issues. However, because Neil is stricken by anxiety and worry (quite overwhelmed by worry in fact), let's ask him to take another step in the Downward Arrow Technique.

So we tell him, "OK, let's imagine that what you fear turns out to be correct, this situation actually happens, and the boss really thinks that you are incompetent. So tell us, what do you worry will be the outcome, what do you think will happen next?" Let us therefore proceed with the Downward Arrow Technique as shown below:

Negative automatic thoughts (thoughts that automatically cross our mind and that cause us to feel anxious and miserable)	Rational responses to negative automatic thoughts
My boss thinks I am an incompetent salesperson ↓	My boss said that it was my fault that we lost this order. He did not label me as incompetent. There have been occasions when my boss has praised me for my performance as well

(continued)

(continued)

Negative automatic thoughts (thoughts that automatically cross our mind and that cause us to feel anxious and miserable)	Rational responses to negative automatic thoughts
Even if this is true, what does it imply to me? What would happen if this thought was true and correct?	
It means I am an incompetent salesperson because my boss knows better and he has the expertise to judge me	My boss may evaluate some of my actions with regard to how they aid in achieving the organization's goals, and he may know certain strengths and weaknesses of mine as a salesperson. However, that does not give him (or anyone in the world) the knowledge, wisdom or capability to evaluate me in entirety and put sweeping, global labels on me such as "incompetent". Besides, I am not incompetent as a salesperson. My past achievements do count – I have successfully closed many sales deals in the past
↓	
Even if this is true, so what? What does it imply to me?	
That means I am an absolute failure	Even if I am not very good as a salesperson, that does not mean I am an utter, absolute, total failure. There have been occasions where I have made good sales deals. I am not always failing and doing bad things! It's not that I cannot learn from my mistakes! Moreover, I have many strengths, talents and interests outside my job. There are a few subjects like astronomy, literature, history and music about which I know quite a bit (in fact, much more than my boss or many of my colleagues). So how am I an utter, total failure? Definitely I am not one
↓	
Even if this is true, what would be the consequences? What does it imply to me? Why would it be so hurtful to me?	

(continued)

(continued)

Negative automatic thoughts (thoughts that automatically cross our mind and that cause us to feel anxious and miserable)	Rational responses to negative automatic thoughts
All my colleagues and even my competitors' salespeople would get to know about my failure	Even my colleagues make mistakes from time to time. Even they do not get certain orders. Even they lose certain accounts. What a ridiculous idea! I make one error and I think that everyone – even my competitors' salespeople – get to know about it! Surely, I am not so important a person –surely, my failure is not so important an event that everyone will be talking about it? Moreover, most of the time people are absorbed in thinking about their own problems
↓	
Even if this is true, what does it imply to me? Why would it be so distressing to me?	
I would become a laughing stock. Everyone would laugh at me behind my back	This is not true. There have been many occasions when my colleagues have made mistakes. I or even the others have never got together and had a good laugh over such things. So why am I judging myself so harshly? Moreover, even if they laugh at me, it doesn't matter. I am worthy, no matter what. There is absolutely no evidence anywhere that my worth or value is determined by my achievements
↓	
Even if this is true, what would happen then? What does it imply to me?	
It means I am worthless. I am useless	I know that I am neither worthless nor useless. There is no definition of human usefulness or worth anywhere. And surely, nowhere does it say that MY PERFORMANCE AT WORK = MY INTRINSIC WORTH OR VALUE AS A HUMAN
↓	
Even if this is true, what does it imply or mean to me?	

(continued)

(continued)

Negative automatic thoughts (thoughts that automatically cross our mind and that cause us to feel anxious and miserable)	Rational responses to negative automatic thoughts
I might be thrown out of my company	My company has never thrown out people for occasional failures. It is expected that human beings will have occasional failures
↓	
Even if this is true, what does it imply to me? What would be so frightful about that?	
I might never get another job in my city or in any other city or area in my country because everyone knows what a total failure I am. Word spreads very fast nowadays, thanks to the extraordinary development of telecommunications. Prospective employers in another city may also come to know that I was kicked out of my job	This is not correct, either. In fact, this is outrageous. It is absurd that my entire city or all the cities in my country or my entire country as a whole would come to know of my dismissal. There are so many different kinds of jobs in so many organizations that I could apply to, even if they are not as lucrative as I would like. It might take some effort and time on my part though
↓	
Even if this is true, what does it imply or mean to me? What would happen if the scenario I fear turns out to be correct?	
I will be unemployed. I will feel terrible. I may go insane.	What is the evidence for this line of thinking? So many people lose jobs… hardly anybody goes insane! On what basis am I thinking that I will succumb to insanity? I might feel "healthily" sad for a while and that's natural. Even if I do go beyond being "healthily sad" and succumb to depression, it would not be a character or behavioural flaw of mine. This is because I would not be consciously or purposely trying to welcome depression into my life. Nobody wants to feel depressed. Most importantly, depression or any other mental illness that I may succumb to can be treated and cured. Anyway, many unfortunate events have some good in them. Hence, this might be an opportunity to really think hard and try to do something different, maybe a completely new career which I would enjoy more. Furthermore, while I am searching for a new job, I can use the time gap to pick up or improve upon some enjoyable, value-adding skills!

So what are the *dysfunctional beliefs* that are emerging from this exercise? Let's have a look. These are:

- My worth or value as a human is determined by my performance, my achievements and my success.
- Others have the wisdom, competence and expertise to label me as a "total failure" and judge my worth.
- If my boss (or my boss's boss or co-workers or anyone else) criticizes me, he is definitely right, definitely accurate.
- I am an absolute and total failure if I am not successful at all times.
- I have to be perfect to gain others' approval. I have to succeed at everything I do in order to gain others' and even my own approval. If I am imperfect and do not succeed at everything I do, I will be scorned and severely disapproved of.
- My worth or value depends on others' approval. Hence, their disapproval will mean that I am worthless.

These are the dysfunctional beliefs that are revealed by the Downward Arrow Technique and that have to be challenged. They are totally unrealistic, illogical and self-defeating and make us vulnerable to depression, mood swings and anxiety. They have to be challenged and rational responses substituted so as to make us feel better in the TRUE sense of the word. For example, when we fail in something and feel inferior, labelling ourselves as failures, we behave as if all our past successes become nullified since we did not succeed this particular instance. This is completely irrational. One way of altering these kinds of deeply entrenched dysfunctional beliefs is to regularly do things for pleasure and not for what they will achieve. In addition, we must frequently make mental notes of all our strengths and past successes.

As an aside and in the context of Neil's example above, it is important to mention here that depression or any other mental illness is just that – an illness – there is nothing to be ashamed about it. The cause of depression and other mental illnesses are yet unknown. The causes may be genetic, biochemical (perhaps caused by hormonal problems), environmental and social and may depend on how we have been raised, our life experiences so far and perhaps many other reasons which scientists are yet to find out. We never do anything deliberately and intentionally to invite depression or other mental illnesses into our lives – we don't want to bring about the feelings of depression. They are not happy feelings. Hence, there are no reasons for us to feel humiliated, embarrassed, mortified, feel like a failure or blame ourselves if we have depression or any other mental illness. Most importantly, after being cured of depression, people become as effective as before.

Returning to dysfunctional beliefs, the question that arises is how does one challenge dysfunctional beliefs? One has to challenge dysfunctional beliefs by looking for objective, impartial evidence that the dysfunctional belief is true or correct and then looking for objective, impartial evidence that it is false or incorrect. Then one is in a position to make a reasoned assessment and decision as to whether it is rational and realistic to continue holding the dysfunctional belief. If the person does not think it's rational and realistic, then he can begin to look for alternative beliefs that fit better with the evidence. It is important to note that rationally and realistically countering our

NATs help us to feel better, while refuting our dysfunctional beliefs in the same manner helps us fortify the path to mental peace at an even deeper and more lasting level. As an example, let us take the case of a person who has a dysfunctional belief that "Human relations are painful". Evidence in favour of and supporting this belief may be that the person had traumatic experiences during his childhood and youth – perhaps his father was violent, an alcoholic and abusive; maybe he was severely ridiculed and bullied at school. Experiences in his adult life may further strengthen the dysfunctional belief – the dominating, bullying boss at work, or the colleague whom he trusted but who turned out to be a backbiter. Evidence against and not supporting the belief that "Human relations are painful" could be that his mother and aunts were kind, supportive and loving and that he had a few friends at college who were nice as well. Perhaps some of his co-workers now are helpful, pleasant and friendly, and the boss anyway is well known for being rude, bad-tempered, mean and unfeeling towards all his subordinates, not only him.

With evidence of this type compiled and analysed both "for" and "against" the dysfunctional belief, the person can weigh it up, assess it and arrive at a judgement. In this specific example, the evidence may seem more or less evenly balanced both "for" and "against" his belief. Therefore, the person may decide not to completely reject his original belief, but modify and mitigate it somewhat. He may conclude that the thought "some human relations are painful, but some are not" better depicts and fits the evidence. Living life with this new rational, revised belief will enable the person to have less emotional troubles and feel better realistically. Another common belief that comes up whenever we are lying in bed but sleep is just not coming is "If somehow I don't get a solid, full night's sleep, I will not be able to work well in office tomorrow". This is incorrect. If we look back, we will find that in the past, we had gone to office after sleepless nights and though we may not have felt physically too good (which we could tolerate), we did maintain the quality of our work. The takeaway here is that instead of worrying about whether we can work the next day, it's better to challenge our distorted, unrealistic thinking and do things like listen to soothing music, watch television, read something, mentally pray or chant – in short, do whatever works for us till sleep comes. We may also close our eyes and just rest and relax in bed instead of agonizing over sleep not coming. This often works and actually helps us to fall asleep, even though it doesn't matter even if we don't. Similarly, when we experience social anxiety, we often think that the people we are talking to (interacting with or giving a lecture or speech to) can discern that we are nervous and tense. This makes us even more anxious. However, these are our inaccurate, distorted thoughts. Usually, people who are observing us cannot make out that we indeed are feeling anxious. In this regard, it is important to mention that when we are giving a presentation (or a talk) and are feeling nervous, it helps to concentrate on the subject matter of our presentation instead of the audience's attitude. This serves to decrease our anxiety. Also, we must remember that we don't HAVE TO make a good presentation. It's not a MUST. We only prefer to make a good presentation. This attitude further helps to decrease our tension.

A note of caution should be struck here. Our dysfunctional beliefs have been deeply etched and ingrained in us since years – perhaps from our early childhood.

This makes them an integral, intrinsic part of us, and therefore, it is quite difficult to eradicate them. One of the fundamental tenets of cognitive therapy is that no matter how well we understand our dysfunctional beliefs, insight alone is not sufficient and will rarely lead to change. We may of course feel better knowing why we are unhappy, because an understanding and knowledge of the situation gives the impression of a feeling of relief and of being curative. However, it is unlikely that we will actually stay better and maintain our improved mental condition unless we make it a habit to repeatedly challenge our negative thoughts and replace them with more rational and realistic ones.

A highly effective cognitive behavioural technique involves testing our negative prophecies with real-life experiments. For instance, I may think that "I am feeling so sad (or bored), that I cannot concentrate on doing any writing". To test this, I can try to start by writing two lines. I can then repeat the test with five lines. I may however tell myself "I will not be able to write more than these five lines". Again, to test this hypothesis out, I may see if I can write one whole paragraph. These experiments often serve to break and dispel the myths of our powerful negative cognitions. Another common but wrong perception that we have is we feel that we have to do something perfectly in order to enjoy it. This is not correct at all. We can actually test this out by keeping a record of the things we do, how perfectly (or efficiently) we think we do them and the pleasure they give us. Often we will see that we get a lot of satisfaction from doing things that we are not experts at and do not feel too satisfied doing things over which we have achieved mastery.

Changing dysfunctional beliefs is a difficult and sometimes long process, but it is definitely not impossible! Of course, changing our ways of thinking requires hard work and practice. We must not forget that these beliefs weren't formed in a day. Nor were they formed overnight. They took years of constructing, practicing, instilling and ingraining them into our psyche. However, it is also true that identifying our negative thinking patterns is the first step towards letting them go. The principle is that if we change our thinking, our moods and state of mind will change and gradually over time and with practice, our thinking and life will begin to change for the better. It is also true that we should expect to backslide now and then, disturb ourselves from time to time and fall back to our irrational ways of thinking, even when we are dealing with familiar issues, the likes of which we had confronted with and dealt with in the past. This is something we can certainly expect, and when the backsliding occurs, we can apply the same processes and methods (to dispute and alter our irrational beliefs) which worked successfully for us in the past and which helped us feel better.

Recapitulation of CT and REBT

To make a long story short, all human beings strive to remain alive, to avoid harm and pain and to achieve happiness. However, it is also true that humans are prone to adopting irrational beliefs and behaviours which stand in the way of their achieving peace and fulfilment. These irrational beliefs riddled with cognitive errors are unrealistic, unreasonable, dogmatic, rigid, extreme, demanding, and exaggerating and include "MUSTs", "SHOULDs", "HAVE TOs" or "OUGHTs"; they are in stark opposition to rational and flexible desires, wishes, preferences and wants. For example, "I SHOULD or MUST always be brave and strong" and "I SHOULD or MUST always be calm and confident". These irrational ways of thinking lead to unhealthy negative emotions such as intense prolonged sorrow, gloom, depression, anxiety and guilt. For instance, someone's thinking after going through a loss might be "It is painful that this loss happened to me, although there is no actual reason why it SHOULD not or MUST not have happened. However, it is not terrible, things could have been worse and I can survive." Another person may think "This absolutely SHOULD not or MUST not have occurred, and it is TERRIBLE/HORRIBLE/AWFUL that it did. The situation is now unbearable, this is the last straw and I will not be able to survive". The first person will experience a healthy feeling of grief, while the second person's thought process may lead him to depression.

To summarize, cognitive behavioural therapy (CBT – the umbrella term for CT and REBT together) asserts that we have the power to change our ways of thinking and thereby radically change the condition of our emotional health. CBT is a profound life-changing philosophy in that a person changes his basic outlook and gives up those MUSTs, SHOULDs, OUGHTS, HAVE TOs and demands and just resorts to having preferences. For example, "I would like to perform very well but I never HAVE TO"; "It would be wonderful if you treat me warmly, kindly and nicely, but there's no reason why you MUST or SHOULD do so". If a person does this he will rarely make himself anxious, miserable or depressed.

Chapter 5
Cognitive Behavioural Therapy (CBT) in the Workplace

How Can Cognitive Behavioural Therapy Techniques (CBT) Help Us in the Workplace?

Dictionaries often define workplace simply as "a place where work is done". However, this definition of workplace can certainly be enriched. In an economy increasingly relying on "knowledge workers", work is done anytime and anywhere. It is better if a definition of the modern workplace recognizes this reality. Hence, *workplace* may be defined as "any environment enabling work to be done". This broader definition will make the workplace include situations and places where people interact to exchange knowledge, services and information.

CBT can be used to challenge and overcome workplace stress by realistically and accurately interpreting events at the workplace. Let us illustrate this with classic adverse situations that we face in the workplace. In the case of each situation, some typical cognitive errors have been mentioned in parentheses.

Trying Situations Which We Face in the Workplace and Which Make Our Stress Go Through the Roof

Situation 1: Facing Criticism

Situation 1

A. *Activating Adverse Event*

- I made a presentation today in the board meeting where the entire senior management was present. There were a few very harsh criticisms about my presentation.

K. Choudhury, *Managing Workplace Stress: The Cognitive Behavioural Way*,
DOI 10.1007/978-81-322-0683-5_5, © Springer India 2013

B. *Irrational Thought(s) I Have About A*

- I really messed up big time. I am no good. I am worthless (MENTAL FILTER, BLACK-AND-WHITE THINKING, MINIMIZATON, MAGNIFICATION, LABELLING).

C. *Consequences of Having Those Thoughts About A*

- Feeling downright miserable

D. *Dispute the Irrational Thoughts in B*

- Where is the evidence that I am a perfect human being who cannot make mistakes?
- Why am I thinking that my performance has to be either extremely good or extremely bad? Can it not be moderately good?
- Just because my presentation was not up to my expectations, how does it make me worthless or valueless? In fact, how is my worthiness or value as a human related to my accomplishments or achievements?

E. *Effective New Thinking: Substitute Something Realistic and Rational Instead of B*

- It is unrealistic to expect that everyone's views would be the same as mine.
- Nowhere does it say that I MUST make a good impression. Thinking like that just puts pressure on me. It's not possible for everybody, for all and sundry, to like me or my work all the time. If they do so, great. If they don't, the world won't come to a screeching halt.
- Even though there were criticisms, there were some points which were appreciated as well. So how can I label my performance as bad? Moderately good would be the right descriptor for my performance. I have definitely not messed up. In fact, am I paying attention to only the dark side of things? Am I focusing only on the criticisms and not remembering the few appreciative remarks regarding my presentation?
- Just because my performance was not as expected, it doesn't make me useless or worthless. What is the definition of usefulness, worth or value anyway in the human context? These are just ideas, just notions and concepts, that's all they are. What is the proof or evidence that human worth (or the value of a human) and accomplishments are equal? How do we measure human worth (or value), and how do we measure accomplishment? And how do we equate the two? What would be the criteria for measuring them? What would be the basis, standards or units for measuring human worth (or value) and accomplishment? There is no answer and there can be no answer. So, I am definitely not worthless (or useless or valueless) because worth (or value) and accomplishments have no relation. I must never feel that "I am inadequate unless I am successful". Adequacy and success are not equal.
- Some of my colleagues have accomplished a lot, but they are ill-mannered, rude, self-centred and aggressive. So do I consider them worthy or valuable?

On the other hand, there are some colleagues and subordinates who are not in high positions, who have not achieved a lot, but who are caring, warm, friendly and a pleasure to be around with. So do I consider them worthless, valueless and useless? This shows that it is highly ridiculous to equate success and accomplishments with human worth or value.

- I'm too hard on myself. I don't always succeed, but I often do. Others have complimented me on my work from time to time. It's when I try to be perfect (which is impossible to be) that I feel stressed, anxious, overwhelmed and disappointed with myself.
- When I aim for perfection, I get too focused on the outcome. This makes me anxious and my work naturally suffers. From now on, I will try to concentrate only on the work by giving steady sincere efforts and not focus on the outcome. That way, I will enjoy my work more instead of feeling tense about it. I will be able to work better, and the quality of the work is bound to improve. The outcome as we all know depends on so many things which are not in my control – organizational politics, subjectivity, favouritism, the mood of the people evaluating me, their personality, their stakes in my work, how they view things, the evaluation criteria, the subjectivity of it and so on. So there's no point evaluating my success based on the outcome of my work. The outcome is totally outside my control. From today onwards, I will rate myself as successful if I give consistent, honest and sincere efforts in any work or project that I do, no matter what the outcome, no matter what the result. My sincere efforts are the only things in my control.
- I can of course think hard about the criticisms that were raised and see if they have some merit and if I can learn something from them. Perhaps I can revisit certain issues.
- I do not have to be perfect. It's not possible to be perfect. I don't need to be perfect.

Result: Feeling less miserable

Situation 2: The Abusive Boss

Situation 2

A. *Activating Adverse Event*

- The boss shouted at me in office today in front of all my colleagues. He was screaming and was really abusive and rude.

B. *Irrational Thought(s) I Have About A*

- My boss SHOULD not have shouted at me like that (Using SHOULD).
- I feel a deep sense of shame to be shouted at in front of others (PERSONALIZATION).

C. *Consequences of Having Those Thoughts About A*

- Intense feeling of hurt
- Feeling insulted
- Feeling angry

D. *Dispute the Irrational Thoughts in B*

- On what basis am I saying that my boss SHOULD not have shouted at me? Do I own him? Do I possess him? Is he my property? If not, then how can I expect him to behave the way I want him to?
- Are my boss and myself the same people that I can expect his behaviour to conform to my standards?
- Is he under my control?

E. *Effective New Thinking: Substitute Something Realistic and Rational Instead of B*

- I feel bad that my boss shouted at me and would have preferred that he had behaved in a civil manner. However, I definitely cannot say that he SHOULD not have shouted at me, since he is an individual whom I do not possess or own or control. It is unrealistic for me to think that his behaviour SHOULD conform to my preferences.
- My boss's behaviour is based on his value systems and principles, which are of course different from mine, since we are two different people. I cannot expect him to behave according to my principles, since he is not me. From where he is coming, he probably thinks that shouting at subordinates is acceptable.
- Even though I would prefer that people do not treat me unkindly, there is no reason that they MUST not do so.
- There is no reason as to why I must feel ashamed by my boss's behaviour. I am not responsible for his behaviour. He is not under my control. How he chooses to react and behave is absolutely his choice. My boss could have handled this situation differently. However, he was the one who chose to behave repulsively in this case. He was the one who lost his temper and was abusive. I have nothing to feel humiliated about. There is no reason for me to blame myself or feel disgraced and mortified.
- My boss's behaviour does not make me any less worthy or less valuable as a person. There is no proof that intrinsic human worth or value equals "not getting abused".
- It's sad that people sometimes misbehave. However, humans are not perfect and that is the unfortunate reality. I must accept the fact that human beings behave well sometimes and badly at other times. Sometimes they behave kindly, sometimes cruelly, sometimes fairly, sometimes unfairly, sometimes politely, sometimes rudely, sometimes selfishly, sometimes unselfishly, some-

times they are obnoxious and mean and sometimes they are friendly and understanding. This is because just like me they are human and just like all humans they are imperfect. Maybe I will talk to my boss later, when he has cooled down, and tell him that I felt pained by his behaviour.

Result: Feeling less angry and hurt and no more inclined to blame and condemn self

Situation 3: Carelessness

Situation 3

A. *Activating Adverse Event*

- The report that I had sent to my boss's boss had two gross mistakes, which were pointed out to me by the big man himself.

B. *Irrational Thought(s) I Have About A*

- My reputation is at stake. Top management will think that I am sloppy with my work and no good (FORTUNE TELLING, MIND READING, MAGNIFICATION, LABELLING, MENTAL FILTER, BLACK-AND-WHITE THINKING).

C. *Consequences of Having Those Thoughts About A*

- Anxious, worried and guilty

D. *Dispute the Irrational Thoughts in B*

- Am I a perfect human being who cannot make gross mistakes ever?

E. *Effective New Thinking: Substitute Something Realistic and Rational Instead of B*

- I cannot avoid making "gross mistakes" at least some of the time, since I am not a perfect human being. In fact, nobody is. It's simply not possible for anyone to get everything right all the time.
- I know I didn't do the report as well as I would have liked to. That doesn't mean that it was totally bad. There were some essential points that I did manage to convey. It was not disastrous. I would have preferred not to have made those gross mistakes though, and it is okay to feel disappointed.
- Others do have the right to point out my mistakes occasionally, and I can be okay with that. I can learn from my errors and mistakes. However, they are just that – some mistakes which I made since I am an imperfect human like them. Others' disapproval has nothing to do with my worth or value as a human, because human value or worth are not measured by the yardsticks of approval and disapproval.

- I will try to learn the lesson here and be more careful next time. In fact, from now onwards, I will check my reports thoroughly a couple of times before sending them across. If I perceive failures and mistakes as opportunities to learn and make my life better, then I may not be so remorseful about or afraid of them.

Result: A much calmer, solution-oriented attitude

It is worth mentioning here that if you have made mistakes and know that you are going to be caught and censured, it's always smarter to admit your mistakes immediately and apologize profusely, instead of defending yourself. You can denounce and blame yourself to your heart's content (please do so) – trust me, criticizing your own self is much better than being criticized by your boss or anyone else. It's much less stressful than trying to argue with your opponents, trying to defend yourself or listening to them denounce you. When you self-accuse and self-blame, you rob others off the opportunity to criticize you – you dispel their clouds of anger. Once you start criticizing your own self, your opponents will have no option but to soften down. They will pardon you and perhaps even assert that your mistakes were not that gross (even though they were). Why would they do this? They would do this because it would give them a "moral high", an opportunity to demonstrate their high moral values, a feeling of being in the dominating position, a feeling of importance, feelings which all human beings want. This almost always works.

Situation 4: Conflicting Values

Situation 4

A. *Activating Adverse Event*

- I see rampant dishonesty in my office. I see my colleagues in Sales and Marketing accepting bribes from customers. I see the Purchase folks accepting bribes from the suppliers, and I see almost everybody inflating their conveyance and miscellaneous expenses. It's extremely disturbing.

B. *Irrational Thought(s) I Have About A*

- Honesty is a quality that I highly value and which I feel that everyone SHOULD have. Without honesty, a person is no longer human. People MUST not be dishonest (Using SHOULD and MUST; LABELLING).

C. *Consequences of Having Those Thoughts About A*

- Emotionally very disturbed
- Disillusioned

D. *Dispute the Irrational Thoughts in B*

- Where is it written that because I think honesty is such a big thing, everybody has to give the same degree of importance to honesty? Is there a global binding rule regarding this?
- Honesty is a particular trait of someone's personality. I know that human beings are complex creatures with many traits. So how can I judge a person in entirety on the basis of his dishonesty, that is, one trait, and label him as bad? Maybe he has other traits and behaviours that are good?
- Moreover, can I expect that a person's value system will be exactly similar to mine?

E. *Effective New Thinking: Substitute Something Realistic and Rational Instead of B*

- Even though I would like people around me to be honest, I cannot demand that everyone will be so, since they are not under my ownership or control. Everybody's values will not be the same as mine.
- The world is not full of perfect people with perfect value systems. If I try to be perfectionistic with regard to others' moral values or even my own moral values, then I will definitely be unhappy. This is because perfection with regard to anything, even moral values, is impossible, unattainable and unrealistic.
- There is no universal standard of honesty that everyone must meet. I cannot expect everyone I work with to have the same level of honesty – that is impossible and absurd. We are all different people. People's values like honesty are shaped by their genes, the way they have been brought up and their life experiences so far. So how can I expect all people to have exactly the same level of honesty that I have? This is a ridiculous expectation on my part.
- There is no rule that says that things have to be the way I want them to be. It hurts, but I can stand it. In fact, I am standing it.
- Perhaps I can concentrate on the positive aspects of my job if I want to remain in this job.

Result: Feeling less disturbed and less disillusioned

Situation 5: No Friends in the Office

Situation 5

A. *Activating Adverse Event*

- In a workshop organized by my office, many of my colleagues were chatting in groups. Though they were inviting others to come and join them, they did not ask me. I felt left out. I have no friends in office.

B. *Irrational Thought(s) I Have About A*

- They do not like me enough to invite me to their group (MIND READING, EMOTIONAL REASONING).
- I MUST have friends in office. You NEED friends in office (Using MUSTs and NEEDs).
- I am not likeable (PERSONALIZATION, LABELLING).

C. *Consequences of Having Those Thoughts About A*

- Feeling depressed
- Low self-esteem

D. *Dispute the Irrational Thoughts in B*

- Am I sure that each and every one of my colleagues in these "groups" dislike me? Am I confusing my feelings with facts? Am I jumping to conclusions?
- Could it be that there are a few who like me but are not calling me because they are exhibiting what is depicted in social psychology as diffusion of responsibility in groups? In the sense that, each person in a group uses others' behaviour as cues to act. To put it in another way, since I was not called initially, it was kind of setting up a chain reaction, and others were not calling me as well.
- Is it necessary to have friends in office?
- On what basis am I saying that I NEED friends in office?

E. *Effective New Thoughts and Beliefs: Substitute Something Realistic and Rational Instead of B*

- It would be nice if I had some friends in office, but if that isn't so, so be it. I will try to be kind and considerate with others, fulfil my duties responsibly and sincerely and try to get the maximum pleasure out of it.
- Most importantly, I certainly don't NEED friends. Not in office, not anywhere. I would prefer to have friends, but I definitely don't NEED friends. I NEED oxygen, water, shelter, food, medicines and clothing. I don't NEED friends. I just prefer to have friends.
- While it would be unpleasant to be without friends, it will not be something terrible.
- There's no evidence that I am not likeable. I have quite a few friends and acquaintances outside office who like me. I have family members who like me a lot as well.
- If my colleagues don't like me, it doesn't diminish my value or worth in any way. Nowhere does it say that your value or worth as a human is equal to the number of friends you have. Hence, I am not valueless or worthless (or less valuable and worthy) if I am unpopular. I can of course try to be pleasant, understanding and caring with people. I can try to improve my social skills. That would increase the probability of my co-workers being nice to me in return and building some good friendships.
- Approval, friendship and love, though they may be desirable, are not absolute necessities. I can survive without them.

- Approval really feels nice. However, approval and disapproval are not the proper tools for measuring human worth or value. There were many eminent scientists like Copernicus and Galileo and renowned philosophers who were not approved of (in fact, they were severely disapproved of) during their times (because what they said went against the prevalent beliefs of their times, even though it was the truth). Did this make them less worthy? Less valuable as human beings? Definitely not.

Result: Feeling less depressed and lonely

Situation 6: My Views Not Being Recognized

Situation 6

A. *Activating Adverse Event*

- During our team meeting, I had suggested something that would really have helped the company in the long run. Logically and objectively, it was a brilliant suggestion, but my team mates did not adopt it. They settled for another very mediocre proposal.

B. *Irrational Thought(s) I Have About A*

- I can't stand it when I propose something which will be genuinely good for the company and its people is rejected (CATASTROPHIZATION).
- Others SHOULD see it my way when I propose something great (Using SHOULD).

C. *Consequences of Having Those Thoughts About A*

- Feeling bitter and frustrated

D. *Dispute the Irrational Thoughts in B*

- Where is the proof or evidence that I can't stand it?

E. *Effective New Thoughts and Beliefs: Substitute Something Realistic and Rational Instead of B*

- Am I assuming that my way of looking at things is the only one possible? Since, anyway, I have to abide by my team's decision, let me go along with my teammates and give this "mediocre" idea a try. Who knows? It may not turn out to be that bad. I might even learn something from the process.

- I cannot expect that others SHOULD see things my way since they are independent individuals (not under my possession or control) with their own views and opinions of what works or not.
- It would have been desirable to have my way, but it is ok even if I don't have my way. I can live with it. The very fact that I am sitting here feeling bitter shows that I can stand it. It is not essential to have my way.
- I can never predict with certainty that whatever I suggested would have been the best for the company in the long run. Who knows what problems it might have encountered? There are so many variables outside my control that could have influenced the process and the outcome if my suggestion was operationalized (of course, this is true for all other suggestions as well).

Result: Feeling less sorry for myself

In these kinds of situations, it is important to note that we often suffer from assumptions like "If I am not the centre of attention or if I am not in the limelight, I am not going to enjoy things and feel satisfied". These are assumptions which should be put to the test by us, by asking "what are the evidences for this assumption?" We may attempt to recollect situations or events when we were in the centre of attention and when we were not in the centre of attention. Once we do that, we will often find that on many occasions we did enjoy things even though we were not in the centre of attention and sometimes did not enjoy things at all even though we were in the centre of attention.

Situation 7: People Going Back on Their Words

Situation 7

A. *Activating Adverse Event*

- I have an important personal commitment tomorrow. My boss agreed last week that he would give me leave for that. Now he is saying that I have to come to office tomorrow (for some work that definitely could have been done later) and that he had never agreed to let me take leave. What a damn liar! It's unfair! This is exceeding all limits. Simply unacceptable.

B. *Irrational Thought(s) I Have About A*

- I can't tolerate being lied to. I can't stand it (CATASTROPHIZATION).
- My boss SHOULD stick to his word and not go back on it. Otherwise, it's unfair (Using SHOULD, EMOTIONAL REASONING).

- It's horrible for a boss to tell lies (CATASTROPHIZATION).
- I SHOULDn't have to come tomorrow (Using SHOULD).

C. *Consequences of Having Those Thoughts About A*

- Feeling extremely angry
- Argumentative
- Feeling cheated, as if taken advantage of

D. *Dispute the Irrational Thoughts in B*

- Where is the evidence that I can't tolerate being lied to? Where is the proof that I cannot take it?
- Who says that a boss MUST stick to his word? Where is it written?
- Where is the evidence that it's horrible for a boss to tell lies?
- What is the foundation for saying that my boss's behaviour is unfair?
- Where does it mention that I SHOULDn't have to come tomorrow?

E. *Effective New Thoughts and Beliefs: Substitute Something Realistic and Rational Instead of B*

- There is no evidence that I can't stand being lied to. The fact that I'm still alive and feeling extremely angry proves that I can stand being lied to.
- Being lied to will not kill me. It is inconvenient and I will have to change my plans, but it's definitely not fatal.
- If I want my boss to behave fairly, then I must understand that he is behaving very fairly, even though I hate it. He is being fair according to his own set of standards and values, not mine. His standards, principles and values are clearly and obviously different from mine. Fairness is something very subjective, and I am sure that my boss believes that his behaviour and actions (which I intensely dislike) are reasonably just and fair.
- There is no proof that a boss has to stick to his word. If there was a universal rule, law or requirement that all bosses have to stick to their words, then my boss would have done so. Since he went back on his word, it is clear that no such rule exists.
- It's not written anywhere that I SHOULDn't have to come tomorrow. I am not the one who makes the rules in this office, even though I'd like to. It's of course disgusting that my boss blatantly lied to me. Since it will not be possible for me to spend the entire day in office tomorrow, because of my urgent personal commitments, I will have to think of some excuse to not come to office or perhaps come later in the day or leave early or whatever. Implementing all those excuses will be very tiresome, but it's not devastating. I can continue to function.
- In future, whenever my boss promises something, I will keep a backup plan ready in case he goes back on his word, or does something else that causes me inconvenience, so that my sufferings are minimized.

Result: Relatively more unruffled and solution-focused

Situation 8: Saying Something Foolish

Situation 8

A. *Activating Adverse Event*

- Today in our monthly meeting, I said a foolish thing. The moment I said it, I realized my goof up. Everyone laughed at me.

B. *Irrational Thought(s) I Have About A*

- I am a fool (MENTAL FILTER, LABELLING, BLACK-AND-WHITE THINKING).
- Being laughed at is terrible/horrible (CATASTROPHIZATION).

C. *Consequences of Having Those Thoughts About A*

- Feeling a deep sense of shame

D. *Dispute the Irrational Thoughts in B*

- Just because I did or said something foolish, what makes me a fool in totality? Am I always doing foolish things? Am I always saying foolish things?
- On what basis am I thinking that being laughed at is terrible/horrible?

E. *Effective New Thoughts and Beliefs: Substitute Something Realistic and Rational Instead of B*

- I said a foolish thing and I wish I had not. However, as an imperfect human being (everyone is), I know that I cannot avoid saying or doing "foolish things" from time to time.
- I know that human beings are complex creatures, with numerous traits. So, how can I judge and label myself foolish in totality, by one foolish thing that I said or did? I may have said or done a foolish thing but that does not make me a fool! My essence, my self, is not defined by any particular act. In reality, when I take a close look at my behaviour, there's no evidence that I act foolishly all the time. In fact, everyone – I repeat, everyone – says foolish things and behaves foolishly on occasions.
- Being laughed at is unpleasant. However, it's not horrible or terrible. Things could have been worse.

- Importantly, most people will not even remember what I said. They will be too busy thinking about themselves, their problems and their lives.

Result: Feeling more in control of myself and feeling better about myself

Situation 9: No Promotion Yet Again

Situation 9

A. *Activating Adverse Event*

- Yet once again, I have been passed over for a promotion.

B. *Irrational Thought(s) I Have About A*

- It is awful. Simply terrible (CATASTROPHIZATION).
- I can't stand it. It's so unfair (CATASTROPHIZATION).
- All the time, things go badly for me (OVERGENERALIZATION).

C. *Consequences of Having Those Thoughts About A*

- Intense, deep frustration

D. *Dispute the Irrational Thoughts in B*

- Where is the evidence that this situation SHOULD not be happening? Where does it say that?
- Where is it written that if I don't get things whenever I want them or right away it's awful?
- Why MUST I get a promotion?
- Where does it say that it will be disastrous if I don't get a promotion? What is the proof?
- Where is the evidence that I can't stand it?
- On what grounds am I saying that the world MUST be fair?

E. *Effective New Thoughts and Beliefs: Substitute Something Realistic and Rational Instead of B*

- I would really have liked to get this promotion, but it is certainly not awful if I have to wait for it. Things could have been worse. I could have been out of a job. It's just very disappointing.
- I obviously don't HAVE to get a promotion, though that would be highly preferable – however, it is just that, a preference. A preference is not a

necessity. It will not be disastrous if I don't get a promotion – it's not the end of the world.

- I certainly can stand it. The very fact that I am brooding over this shows that I am standing it and can stand it.
- Even though I would like it to be so, I cannot demand that the world be a fair place. Unfortunately, I do not make the laws and rules of the world.
- Maybe I can start thinking of looking for another job or moving to another department or function, where the chances of career advancement would be better?
- Life can be enjoyable even if I don't get salary increases or promotions. I can reasonably enjoy my life even if I stay in this job till I retire. It will definitely not kill me to be in this job. There are multiple things that give me gratification like my hobbies (going to the gym, hiking, playing the guitar, dancing, basketball), hanging out with my friends and my other social relations. These make up for the happiness that I don't get at work. There is no decree that you have to get all your contentment and your life's fulfilment from your workplace.
- Why am I saying "everything" goes badly with me? I know I am totally blowing this up out of all proportion. Of course, some things do go badly with me from time to time, just as they do with others, but some things do go well for me as well.

Result: More accepting of the present situation and hence less disappointed

A common dysfunctional belief in this context is "It is useless, pointless and meaningless doing anything because I did not get the promotion or project or job that I badly wanted". This kind of thinking calls for a thorough analysis, where objective, impartial evidence which support and do not support this belief are to be examined.

Situation 10: Failing To Be Assertive

Situation10

A. *Activating Adverse Event*

- During the meeting today, while I was making my presentation, many questions were raised. Some of my senior colleagues were being argumentative for the sake of it. I did not persist in arguing with them, even though I pointed out their fallacies and my views on the issues raised. However, later some of my colleagues told me that I SHOULD have been more assertive and tougher in dealing with these aggressive people. They told me that I should be more confident in general.

B. *Irrational Thought(s) I Have About A*

- I really OUGHT to have been assertive. I SHOULD always be assertive. That's what they taught me in the assertiveness training course I took recently. I just came across as a very weak person to others today (MENTAL FILTER, BLACK-AND-WHITE THINKING, EMOTIONAL REASONING, LABELLING, using SHOULD and OUGHT).

C. *Consequences of Having Those Thoughts About A*

- Feel that I lack confidence
- Feel that I am weak and too docile
- Feel that people can easily trod over me
- Low self-esteem

D. *Dispute the Irrational Thoughts in B*

- Why am I thinking that I was not assertive?
- Is there a law that says I MUST always be assertive?
- Is it possible for a human being to be perfect and therefore assertive 100 % of the time?
- How do I know that being assertive always gives you the best results?
- Why am I thinking that I am not confident?
- What is the evidence that I came across as a weak person?

E. *Effective New Thoughts and Beliefs: Substitute Something Realistic and Rational Instead of B*

- I think I was assertive – being assertive means to state your views in a way that does not hurt anyone else. That is exactly what I did. I was assertive and not aggressive. Being aggressive implies stating your views in a way that hurts, offends or insults others. I am glad that I was not aggressive. That is not what I believe in. It doesn't matter if others are aggressive. I don't HAVE to be like others.
- I would prefer to be more assertive, but I am a human being and therefore not perfect. So it's unrealistic that I will be assertive 100 % of the time.
- There is no evidence that you have to be assertive always. There may be times when being submissive and yielding to others' wishes might be better for me (of course, assuming that the other person is not asking me to do anything that will harm me or anyone else). Who knows? I might actually gain in some way such as learn new things by listening to and giving in to others' wishes. Moreover, sometimes, for issues which are of trifling importance, just going along with the flow and agreeing to cede to others' views may be quite peaceful instead of being assertive. More so, as being assertive may sometimes lead to unnecessary arguments and I know that in an argument nobody wins – each

person emerges more convinced after the argument that he was right all along. Nowhere does it say that I HAVE to be assertive all the time. My coping strategies will have to be flexible in response to the various adversities and provocations that I face. On some occasions, lowering my expectations may be better instead of being assertive.

- I don't HAVE to be an expert in anything. I can of course, try to increase my assertiveness skills. I might sometimes feel uncomfortable when I am trying to act assertive, but with time it will become easier.
- There is no evidence that I came across as a weak person today. Only some of my colleagues raised the "lack of confidence issue". I did not take a survey of all my colleagues to find out what they thought of my attitude during the presentation. Anyway, if people confuse aggressiveness with assertiveness or think that a person can be assertive 100 % of the time, then it's a case of their cognitive errors and unrealistic, irrational and wrong thinking on their part. I need not be bothered about that.
- I am confident with regard to my area of expertise. There is no such thing called being *confident in general*. Nobody can be confident in all areas and activities of their life. That is an unrealistic, perfectionistic attitude. You can only be more confident in some areas, where you have the required knowledge, experience, ability and expertise and less so in other areas where you don't. Even in areas where you do have immense knowledge, experience and expertise, you cannot be 100 % confident – there are things that you don't know and new things to learn as the area continuously evolves.

Result: Feeling realistically confident

Situation 11: Being Alone Is Disheartening

Situation 11

A. *Activating Adverse Event*

- Tonight there is a big celebration party at the office. Spouses or partners of all the employees have also been invited. As usual, my partner is unwilling to go and has practically refused. I would rather stay at home than go alone to the office party.

B. *Irrational Thought(s) I Have About A*

- If I am alone at the party, I will definitely be unhappy and forlorn (FORTUNE TELLING, EMOTIONAL REASONING).
- Going alone to a party without a partner makes me appear as a total loser, as someone weird, as someone who could not get anyone to come with him/her.

My office people will see me as a lonely creature (MIND READING, LABELLING).

C. *Consequences of Having Those Thoughts About A*

- Feeling morose, glum
- Feeling deprived

D. *Dispute the Irrational Thoughts in B*

- On what basis am I thinking that being alone at the party will make me feel so dejected that I would rather not go?
- Where is the evidence that people will think I am a total loser, a weird and lonely soul because I have come to the party alone?

E. *Effective New Thoughts and Beliefs: Substitute Something Realistic and Rational Instead of B*

- Let me just put this to the test – let me go on my own to the party tonight and try it out. Sure, maybe if I had someone to go with that might have been fun. However, let me check out for myself if going on my own is so dreadful? Who knows? Maybe it will be fun. I may be able to stay longer, meet and interact with many more people than if I was towing my unwilling and uninterested partner around? At least, I won't have to worry whether my partner is feeling bored or uneasy at the party. Let me indulge myself tonight and find out if I enjoy it?
- There are no evidences that being alone means being lonely. There are some things we enjoy doing with others, but there are so many things that we enjoy doing alone – like reading a book, relaxing with a cup of hot tea/coffee, listening to music, visiting a museum, browsing through a bookshop, eating something good, surfing the Net, doing exercises, solving puzzles, taking a walk, etc. – can you think of others? The list is extensive. Maybe I can challenge and put to the test my belief that many of my activities would be unpleasant, uninteresting and boring unless I have someone to share them with?
- I really don't know what other people at the party would be actually thinking. I can never find it out – it's just not possible to delve into other people's minds. Moreover, others will think what they wish to. I cannot control their thoughts. It does not matter either. Only my own thoughts can have an effect on how I feel. As long as I do not do anything which I consider inappropriate, I am perfectly within my rights to be there on my own. If someone finds my unaccompanied presence annoying or strange, it's not something that I have to bother about.

Result: Feeling less dependant

Situation 12: Looking Back with Deep Regrets

Situation 12

A. *Activating Adverse Event*

- I have been in this company for 20 years. As I ruminate and look back, I realize once again, that I have not been successful. On the whole, my career has been pretty average. This, even though I have a brilliant academic record. This is really disheartening. I often feel so demoralized.

B. *Irrational Thought(s) I Have About A*

- I MUST be successful. I HAVE to be successful (Using MUST, HAVE TO).

C. *Consequences of Having Those Thoughts About A*

- Depression

D. *Dispute the Irrational Thoughts in B*

- Where is the rule that I MUST be successful?
- Why am I thinking that I HAVE to be successful?

E. *Effective New Thoughts and Beliefs: Substitute Something Realistic and Rational Instead of B*

- I would like to be successful but there is no reason why I MUST be successful.
- Where is the evidence that to be worthwhile or valuable as a human you have to be successful? There is no proof that "worth or value of a human = success achieved". There is no universally accepted definition of human worth or human value and the parameters that contribute to it.
- I can find joy in living even if I am not successful. There are so many activities that I enjoy (travelling, gardening, reading, playing golf, playing chess, spending time with my friends, catching up with my acquaintances). Why am I relying on work to give me all of life's satisfactions?
- Why am I equating success with happiness? The elation that success or achievement gives us is so very fleeting. We all have experienced it – a few days after success, one feels hollow inside as life gets back to square one.
- Why don't I see this as an opportunity and take a hard look at my life? Maybe I can seriously give a good thought to the things that I would like to do and/or the things that I am good at and try my hand there? This could be a new hobby, a new activity or a new career? Perhaps a new part-time career on the side, in a field that I like? It would be really satisfying if I can enjoy what I do. Maybe I can think of learning something new? Maybe I can think of joining a club? Perhaps I can think of building new friendships or strengthening my existing ones? Human interactions can provide a lot of joy – they provide us a platform to learn and discover so many things about life if we care to

listen well. Moreover, they often serve to decrease our stress levels by allowing us to ventilate our frustrations and explore possible ways to cope with them. Maybe I can think of doing some social work? I can also look around for some interesting activity or project; pursue it; give it an honest, sincere, long try; and see if I find it engaging. If I don't find it absorbing, I can look for other fields, other hobbies. I don't HAVE TO stick to one single absorbing interest throughout my life. I can try many things and see which ones give me pleasure! It is a well-known fact that the human brain loves diversity – therefore, if I can have a variety of interests, that's even better.

- Academic brilliance and success are not necessarily correlated. Success in the corporate world (and otherwise also) may depend on many things besides sincere performance – your networking skills, your communication skills, the opportunities you get, organizational politics, favouritism, your gender and of course your luck, to name a few. Moreover, intelligence has many facets. There are people who are academically not brilliant but who are quite intelligent with regard to networking, people-pleasing and social skills. Often, these people shine in the corporate world. It's not possible or even necessary that everyone has all the facets of intelligence sharply honed and shining.
- If I enjoy what I do, nothing will like it. I might achieve success, although it does not matter even if I don't. There is no rule that says I MUST be successful. I don't NEED to be successful. I can try though to enjoy my life and live it fully for my own sake.

Result: Feeling less morose, less demoralized; feeling more positive with a hope-filled outlook

Situation 13: Conflict with Friend

Situation 13

A. *Activating Adverse Event*

- Had a huge conflict with my closest friend at work. Since the fight happened, he has been steadily ignoring me even though I did try to patch things up.

B. *Irrational Thought(s) I Have About A*

- I can't bear it if my friends are not nice to me. This is intolerable (CATASTROPHIZATION).
- I may never have another friend in my life (OVERGENERALIZATION, EMOTIONAL REASONING, FORTUNE TELLING).

C. *Consequences of Having Those Thoughts About A*

- Feeling melancholy
- Feeling lonely
- Feeling rejected

D. *Dispute the Irrational Thoughts in B*

- What is the foundation for saying that the situation is unbearable?
- On what grounds am I saying that I can't bear it if my friends are not nice to me?
- How do I know that I will never have any more friendships in my life?

E. *Effective New Thoughts and Beliefs: Substitute Something Realistic and Rational Instead of B*

- There is no evidence that I absolutely must never face rejection. No rule of the universe says that, because if it did, I would not have been rejected. Since I have been rejected, it clearly shows that no such universal law exists. I am feeling somewhat lonely, but I can definitely take it. I want my friends to be nice to me, but I can stand it if they're not. In fact, I am standing it now, even though I don't like it.
- I can perhaps become absorbed in other causes or pursuits to keep myself mentally busy and overcome my loneliness.
- There is no proof that I will never have any more friends.
- There's no evidence that I am unlikeable as a friend – but even if I were, this proves nothing about my "worth" or "value", since "human worth" or "human value" is not equal to having friends.
- I greatly desire friendship, love, acceptance and approval. They are really nice things. However, they are not absolute necessities. I don't need friends. I can definitely live without friends, even though it might be somewhat unpleasant. Most importantly, I don't need approval. I may want approval, but I can definitely live without it.
- I may attempt to make up with my friend once more. If he still doesn't want me as a friend, I will accept that and try to build other friendships.
- Disapproval from one friend won't lead to disapproval from another friend and then another. It doesn't spread like volcanoes' lava. Conflict with one friend doesn't mean I will end up totally alone, without any friends in my life. Besides, there are other colleagues in my office who seem to like me well enough.
- If I demand that all the significant people in my life MUST like or love me, then I am aiming for perfectionistic goals. We know that in reality perfection is unattainable. If I NEED approval or affection from my colleague or boss or anyone else, I will always be anxious and worrying as to how deep is that affection and how long that approval and affection will last. Most probably, it may not last very long, because to have someone approve me always, I will always have to behave as per how he/she wants me to, which is not humanly possible and which is very strenuous and stressful. I have my moods, my own desires and my own values. Moreover, I may irritate and bore others if I am always trying to catch their attention and please them in order to seek approval. Most importantly, if I NEED others' approval and thus constantly pursue it,

then I will always be trying to lead my life according to others' wishes, as others would want me to. I would become so very other-directed. Do I want that? Or do I want to live life according to my dreams and goals?

Result: Mood has been uplifted

Situation 14: Others Taking Me for Granted

Situation 14

A. *Activating Adverse Event*

- My boss and other superiors are always asking me to help them with their work and do things outside my job boundaries. I find it very hard to refuse. They just take me for granted. They are really difficult and giving me a hard time.

B. *Irrational Thought(s) I Have About A*

- People MUST not take me for granted (Using MUST).

C. *Consequences of Having Those Thoughts About A*

- Feeling used

D. *Dispute the Irrational Thoughts in B*

- What is the evidence that people MUST not take me for granted?
- Is it correct that my boss absolutely MUST not give me a hard time?

E. *Effective New Thoughts and Beliefs: Substitute Something Realistic and Rational Instead of B*

- I would prefer that people do not take me for granted, but there is no compelling reason that they SHOULD not.
- My boss SHOULD give me a hard, difficult time because that is what is happening! Once again, my boss and other superiors are not under my control. Moreover, my views and my superiors' views of what constitutes my job boundary obviously differ – perhaps rightly so, since we are different people! So on what basis can I say that they SHOULD not give me a hard time? What I am going through is, of course, quite inconvenient, but it's not awful – it could be much worse. For example, my boss could have me thrown out of this job by cooking up false stories about me!
- Maybe I can think of politely telling my boss and other superiors that I am overworked and already have too much on my plate? Perhaps I can phrase it

as a request or in a light, humorous manner? Maybe I can seek their advice with regard to handling situations like this? Who knows? Maybe they also went through these kinds of situations in the early part of their careers! Perhaps I can even take the advice of co-workers whom I respect and trust?
- Maybe I can attempt to prioritize things (do the urgent, important things first) and sharpen my discipline and time-management skills to see if the situation can be improved? I can discuss the prioritization with my boss as well to see if we can come to an agreement.
- If worse comes to worst, perhaps I may gradually try to move to a different area in the same company or some other job in some other company?

Result: *Feeling less disturbed and more oriented towards addressing the problem*

Situation 15: Not Keeping My Cool

Situation 15

A. *Activating Adverse Event*

- Today, when one of the guys in office made a cruel joke aimed at me, I got so nervous, upset and angry that my voice started shaking and I began stuttering in front of everyone. A colleague mentioned that I had acted immaturely.

B. *Irrational Thought(s) I Have About A*

- I MUST NEVER display weakness (Using MUST).
- It is horrible to display weakness (CATASTROPHIZATION).
- People SHOULD never be unkind or cruel (Using SHOULD).
- I shouldn't be so upset over such "*trifling, insignificant*" things. It makes me look "*feeble and pathetic*" (Using SHOULD, LABELLING, EMOTIONAL REASONING).
- I should never act immature (Using SHOULD).

C. *Consequences of Having Those Thoughts About A*

- Feeling humiliated and ashamed
- Low self-esteem

D. *Dispute the Irrational Thoughts in B*

- Where does it say that I MUST never display weakness?
- Where is the evidence that it is horrible to display weakness?
- Where is the law that people SHOULD never be unkind or cruel?

- Why am I saying that "I shouldn't be so upset over such *trifling, insignificant* things – it makes me look *feeble* and *pathetic*"? Is there any evidence to back this up?

E. *Effective New Thoughts and Beliefs: Substitute Something Realistic and Rational Instead of B*

- I would prefer not to display weakness, but there is no rule that I MUST not.
- There is no rule that says it is horrible to display weakness. Moreover, it's not horrible. Things could have been even worse – I could have burst into tears.
- My displaying weakness just confirms that I am a human being who is not emotionally perfect. A perfect emotional state is impossible, unrealistic and therefore unattainable. It does not exist. No one can be calm, confident and in control all the time.
- My displaying weakness has nothing to do with my value or worth, since human worth or value is not equal to "not displaying weakness".
- Even though I would prefer people to be kind, I cannot demand that people SHOULD be kind. They can be whatever they wish to. I don't own or possess them. Hence, I can't expect that they will behave according to my desires or standards. Besides, they are different individuals; they are not me. Hence, they will operate according to their own values, principles, desires, self-interests, constraints, inherent nature and moods. Finally, I cannot control other people's behaviour.
- It's regrettable that people sometimes do bad, hurtful things. We all do it. We all say and do mean, cruel and hateful things at times, more so when we ourselves feel angry, hurt or wronged. Humans are not perfect and that is the reality.
- Maybe I will point out to this guy later that I had felt pained by his comments.
- If someone else was upset by any such similar situation, I wouldn't call it *trifling and insignificant*. I would try to be compassionate, caring and help him or her. I certainly wouldn't label that person as *feeble and pathetic*. So why am I being so cruel and harsh on myself? It is worth mentioning here that most of the time we are much more cruel, malicious and mean to our own selves than others are to us. With our irrational, brutal, unkind and self-blaming thoughts directed to our own selves, we on our own make ourselves unhappy – others are not usually as unkind to us.
- Last but not the least, I will behave immaturely every now and then ... everybody does so ... I am not perfect and don't need to be perfect.

Result: Regained my self-respect and feeling better about myself

Situation 16: Just Too Much Work

Situation 16

A. *Activating Adverse Event*
One impossible deadline after another. I am fully overloaded at my workplace. This is just too much.

B. *Irrational Thought(s) I Have About A*

- I MUST not be overloaded (Using MUST).
- I MUST not feel overwhelmed with responsibilities (Using MUST).

C. *Consequences of Having Those Thoughts About A*

- Frustration

D. *Dispute the Irrational Thoughts in B*

- Where is the proof that I MUST not be overloaded? Why am I expecting that I MUST not be overloaded?
- Where does it say that I MUST not be overwhelmed with responsibilities?

E. *Effective New Thoughts and Beliefs: Substitute Something Realistic and Rational Instead of B*

- I would prefer not to be overloaded, but there is no rule that I MUST not be so. Even though I would love to, I don't make the rules in this office.
- Perhaps I can talk to my boss to see if anything can be done about my workload. I can think of prioritizing and better managing my time. I can discuss with my boss my prioritized list of tasks, where I tackle the urgent and important tasks first. Possibly my boss can give fruitful suggestions on how to deal with huge workloads. I can also seek his advice on the possibility of delegating some tasks. In addition, I can think of ways to simplify my work.
- From now onwards, I can try to complete each task as and when it comes up, immediately as it comes up (of course, it depends on the nature of the task) instead of letting it pile up. This will protect me from the worry and angst caused by piled up work.
- It's to my advantage to keep my work goals rational and modest and aim for a reasonable performance in anything I do, instead of aiming for perfectionistic, superlative performances. Perfectionism creates unnecessary stress and pressures and brings about incapacitating fears of failure. This in turn may prevent me from even starting the work. What's more, perfectionistic attitudes (with the associated focus on outcomes) rob me off my resourcefulness, interest, enjoyment and inspiration and hence hamper the quality of work. No wonder the quality of work suffers when we aim for perfectionistic targets! If I keep my goals modest and aim for a reasonable performance, I will find it easier to start and continue with the work. Once I have put in a reasonable performance, I can always revise my work and make it better. In a nutshell, if

I keep my goals modest, the quality of my work and my effectiveness will be higher.

- I can undertake huge, difficult or complex workloads by doing it in small parts. It's not necessary that I have to address a huge workload all at one go. I can aim for say 15–20 min per day to tackle a difficult, complex job. That way, I will feel more motivated to start the work and won't feel inundated by it. Often, I will find that once I commence the work I will feel enthused and able to go on for much longer than 20 min (however, always aim for small time slots). My enthusiasm (thanks to the small time slots I am aiming for) will enable me to churn out higher quality work and increase my effectiveness. Most importantly, I will not be enticed to put off the work since I know that I only have to work for 15–20 min at any given point of time. Of course, I must reward myself (with anything I like) and give myself due credit for each phase of the work completed.
- One technique which is very helpful, when we are mentally distracted and find it difficult to concentrate, is to tackle the work in small time slots. For example, I may decide to read a project report for 5 min and after that permit myself to indulge in my thoughts for say 2 min. After my thinking break gets over, I can again decide to read the report for another 5 min followed by another thinking break. This actually helps to increase our effectiveness. Alternatively, I may decide to complete reading the entire report first (assuming it's not too long) and set time aside for indulging in my thoughts after finishing the reading. These methods also work well for young people who find it difficult to concentrate on their studies. It increases the overall concentration and effectiveness levels.
- With regard to my colossal workload, I can also seek the counsel of some very experienced colleagues whom I respect and whom I trust enough to confide in. If even this doesn't work out, perhaps I might think of changing departments or functions or the organization itself.
- Of course, I must realize that a job with a lower workload level may come with a lower pay, less benefits and less prestige, but that trade-off maybe worth it if my life becomes more peaceful.

Result: Feeling less frustrated and more oriented towards correcting the situation

Situation 17: An Absolutely Vague Job

Situation 17

A. *Activating Adverse Event*

I am in Marketing, but it seems that I am doing all kinds of stuff – ranging from project evaluations, calculating cash flows, making the budget, chalking out performance appraisal parameters – you name it. There are no clear job boundaries, no sharp job definitions. I hate it. I can't stand this uncertainty, this vagueness. It seems I am doing everything save cleaning the carpets.

B. *Irrational Thought(s) I Have About A*

- I can't stand uncertainty or ambiguity (CATASTROPHIZATION).
- I can't stand vagueness of job boundaries (CATASTROPHIZATION).
- This SHOULD not be the case – job boundaries SHOULD be very well defined (Using SHOULD).

C. *Consequences of Having Those Thoughts About A*

- Confused and demotivated

D. *Dispute the Irrational Thoughts in B*

- Where is the evidence that I can't stand uncertainty/ambiguity?
- Where is it written that this situation SHOULD not be happening? Where is the evidence that this situation SHOULD not be taking place?
- Where is the proof that I can't tolerate vague job boundaries?

E. *Effective New Thoughts and Beliefs: Substitute Something Realistic and Rational Instead of B*

- I would prefer to have a job with clear boundaries. I would like to know what exactly is expected from me. However, there's no proof that I can't stand uncertainty, ambiguity or vagueness. In fact, at present, I am putting up with all three.
- There is no reason that this situation SHOULD not be happening. As a matter of fact, it is happening. Once again, much as I would like to, I don't get to design jobs, allocate jobs or make any rules in this office.
- I think I will talk to my boss and request him to clarify just what exactly my job entails and the responsibilities expected of me. I am also going to convey to him that I am having difficulty coordinating such a wide array of disparate jobs. I can seek his advice on this matter. I will convey to him (respectfully, of course, because if I talk to him in a demanding tone, it will make him annoyed, since nobody likes to be forced or dominated; in fact he will not want to help me if I am demanding) that I am uncomfortable with regard to this lack of clarity, this lack of focus and ask him if my concerns could be addressed.

Result: Less annoyed and more focused towards rectifying the problem

Situation 18: An Absolutely Boring Job

Situation 18

A. *Activating Adverse Event*

I find my job to be extremely boring. There are a few interesting moments, but by and large, all day I am teaching students, most of whom are only interested in their final grades and getting a job. It is simply unbearable. It is driving me crazy.

B. *Irrational Thought(s) I Have About A*

- I MUST never feel bored (Using MUST).
- I find it unbearable when I feel bored. I can't tolerate it. It's killing me (CATASTROPHIZATION).
- My job is extremely boring (OVERGENERALIZATION, MENTAL FILTER, MAGNIFICATION).

C. *Consequences of Having Those Beliefs About A*

- Feeling down, listless and demoralized

D. *Dispute the Irrational Thoughts in B*

- Why SHOULD I never feel bored? Where is that written in stone?
- What is the evidence that I MUST never feel bored?
- What is the proof that I can't stand it when I am bored?
- Where is the law or evidence that says that I always HAVE TO do what I wish to do? Where is the proof?
- Is there a rule that I MUST have what I want and wish for? Where is the proof for this? Where does it say this?

E. *Effective New Thoughts and Beliefs: Substitute Something Realistic and Rational Instead of B*

- I would prefer a more interesting job, but there are no grounds for saying that I can't stand boredom. In fact, I am tolerating it. I have not died as yet.
- Nowhere does it say that I HAVE TO do what I wish or want to do. There is no rule that says I MUST never feel bored.
- There is no law or rule that says that I MUST have what I want or wish.
- To be honest, my job is not totally boring. There are certain things I like about my job. There are certain colleagues who are great. Some of the staff are very fun and pleasant as well. I like the physical environment in my office. Most importantly, not all my students are the truant types. There are some who are sincere and serious, who respond well in class and who are appreciative of my efforts. There are some who have a thirst for knowledge and who come up after class to discuss many interesting aspects of the issues I have taught

them. Many of my students have lots of life experience and work experience which they share with me and I enjoy listening to and learning from these. From now on, I will try to focus on the positives of my job. This way, I would feel less disheartened. I will also try to reduce my expectations from my job, so as to decrease my disappointment. After all, no job can be perfect.

- I can find my life rewarding even if I continue to stay in this job. This is because, even though some aspects of my job are boring, my life outside my job gives me gratification. I enjoy my friends, my family and my hobbies (movies, music, reading, cooking, playing tennis). I get pleasure from my creative pursuits like acting and painting. These make up for the fulfilment, stimulation and joy that I don't get at work. There is no rule, law or requirement that says that I MUST get all the contentment, pleasures, excitements, stimulations and satisfactions of life from my work. That would be an unrealistic expectation as well.
- Let me see if I can make my job more interesting. Maybe I can try out new ideas, new methods of teaching and new topics to teach (what with my field continually evolving), which would involve me and the students more and make the classes more interesting for all of us. Of course, this has to be a continuous process to maintain the vibrancy of the experience and keep us all enthused and motivated.

Result: More accepting and tolerant of the present situation and therefore less discouraged. Using boredom as an opportunity to see if work could be made more meaningful and satisfying. Viewing the opulence of life in totality, instead of taking a tunnel view and focusing only on the work aspect of life

Situation 19: Disobedient Subordinates

Situation 19

A. *Activating Adverse Event*

I have repeatedly told my subordinates not to go out for such long smoking breaks during office hours, but to no avail! This is outrageous! They go away for these breaks at least seven times a day!

B. *Irrational Thought(s) I Have About A*

- People MUST live up to my expectations or it is TERRIBLE! (Using MUST, CATASTROPHIZATION)
- I am ineffective as their boss (PERSONALIZATION, BLACK-AND-WHITE THINKING, MENTAL FILTER, LABELLING).

C. *Consequences of Having Those Thoughts About A*

- Extremely irritated, agitated and troubled

D. *Dispute the Irrational Thoughts in B*

- What and how much control do I have over what someone else does or doesn't?
- How can I expect that others MUST live up to my expectations?
- Where is the proof that it is terrible if others do not live up to my expectations?

E. *Effective New Thoughts and Beliefs: Substitute Something Realistic and Rational Instead of B*

- It's irrational to think that I can expect people to be the way I want at all times. When they aren't, it's NOT terrible. It is certainly unpleasant, it's not desirable, but it is not awful, terrible or horrible. Thinking something as awful, terrible or horrible implies that it is 100% bad. To repeat, nothing can be 100 % bad. Things can always be worse.
- I must not forget that my subordinates are adults and that I cannot control or force them to do anything. I can only attempt to persuade and influence them. People anyway do not like to be dominated or forced. Ultimately, my subordinates' behaviour is their choice as thinking adults, their responsibility. I should not unnecessarily blame or condemn myself for their indiscipline.
- There is no evidence that I am ineffective as their boss. It's not that they are always disregarding my instructions. In fact, my subordinates and I have successfully completed many projects together, under my guidance and directive.
- I must bear in mind that my subordinates and I are different people altogether. They are behaving from their own value systems and operating from their own standards and principles of what is acceptable/unacceptable, good/bad, proper/improper conduct.
- I will discuss the matter with my subordinates and see if something can be worked out. Repeating my wishes (even if for the umpteenth time) and reinforcing them may work. If they continue with this behaviour, I may also have to continue repeating my directives from my end, as long as I am able to.
- I may take suggestions from other colleagues in this regard. Maybe some reward/punishment scheme can be worked out? All said and done, smoking is highly addictive and it might be a tricky problem to solve. Perhaps I can think of lowering my expectations in this matter.

Result: Feeling less irritated and less inclined to blame self

Situation 20: No End to Seeking Approval

Situation 20

A. *Activating Adverse Event*

I have tried everything to please my boss. I work smart, I am sincere, I take on much more than most others, yet I see the boss favouring people who are always sweet-talking and flattering him. This is terribly frustrating. It completely demotivates me.

B. *Irrational Thought(s) I Have About A*

- I MUST be approved of or accepted by people I find important (Using MUST).
- People MUST treat me fairly and give me what I NEED (Using MUST and NEED).

C. *Consequences of Having Those Beliefs About A*

- Intense frustration

D. *Dispute the Irrational Thoughts in B*

- Where does it say that I HAVE to be approved of (though I would LIKE to be)?
- Is there any reason why people MUST treat me fairly?
- What is the proof that my boss is treating me unfairly?

E. *Effective New Thoughts and Beliefs: Substitute Something Realistic and Rational Instead of B*

- It is not possible to be approved of or accepted by everyone you want. It just doesn't happen, because it's unrealistic and perfectionistic. Even if I'm not approved of by my boss, I will continue to work sincerely. If he still doesn't approve of me, I will accept it, though I may not like it. If the situation becomes worse and I find it very demotivating, I may think of greener pastures.
- If I want my boss to behave "fairly", then he should behave exactly as he is doing now, even though I do not like it at all. Fairness is something very subjective. My boss is operating from his own standards and behaving "fairly" according to his own standards, principles and values. His views, his ideals and his standards are unfortunately not the same as mine. I cannot expect them to be the same either because my boss and I are two different people.
- Even if I don't get my boss's or anybody else's approval, it does not decrease my intrinsic worth or value as a human even by a grain. I know that human worth or value is not equal to the approval you get.

Result: Feeling less troubled and less disconcerted

Situation 21: Can't Find the Ideal Solution

Situation 21

A. *Activating Adverse Event*

I am stuck with a complex problem. There are some solutions, but I can't zero in on the ideal one. It's damn frustrating.

B. *Irrational Thought(s) I Have About A*

- Each and every problem SHOULD have an ideal, perfect solution (Using SHOULD).

C. *Consequences of Having Those Thoughts About A*

- Feeling bothered and helpless

D. *Dispute the Irrational Thoughts in B*

- How does one define an ideal solution?
- How do I know that an ideal solution exists for all problems?
- What is the evidence that I cannot live with less than the ideal?

E. *Effective New Thoughts and Beliefs: Substitute Something Realistic and Rational Instead of B*

- Problems often have multiple solutions. There may be no way of knowing which the best solution is until a very long time, in the long run, if at all. Let me get on with what I now perceive to be is the best solution. Even if an ideal solution is there, I sure can tolerate and live with less than the ideal. There are no evidences that I cannot. Anyway, the definition of an ideal solution is pretty nebulous. Rationally, there is no such thing called an ideal or perfect solution. Every solution can be improved.

Result: Feeling less exasperated, less confused and moving on

Situation 22: Failed to Meet My Targets

Situation 22

A. *Activating Adverse Event*

I failed to carry out all the urgent, important things that I had planned to do today. It's a disaster. What will I tell the boss?

B. *Irrational Thought(s) I Have About A*

- I SHOULD always carry out everything I plan (Using SHOULD).
- It's a disaster (MAGNIFICATION, EMOTIONAL REASONING).

C. *Consequences of Having Those Beliefs About A*

- Feeling very upset

D. *Dispute the Irrational Thoughts in B*

- Where is the evidence that I always SHOULD carry out everything I plan?
- On what basis am I describing the situation as a disaster?

E. *Effective New Thoughts and Beliefs: Substitute Something Realistic and Rational Instead of B*

- I cannot always hope or expect to complete everything I planned for. I am not perfect. I am fallible, like any other human being. It would have been great if I had finished it all, but the fact that I haven't is definitely not dreadful or disastrous. It could have been worse. I could have accomplished even less today for some reason or the other. In fact, it's natural not to finish all that I have planned for on time, when the work pressure is so high. If my boss comments on this, I will explain the situation to him.

Result: Feeling less upset

Again, it is important to mention that we often suffer from assumptions like "I will not feel satisfied unless I finish everything that I had planned for today. I have to finish everything today. Finishing part of the work will make me feel discontented". This cannot be repeated enough that these are assumptions which should be examined by asking "What is the evidence for this assumption?" and by keeping a track of the times when we did feel fulfilled and happy even though we had finished part of the task. Similar assumptions which need to be tested include "Things won't be pleasurable and satisfying unless I can do them perfectly". If we investigate this assumption, we will see that there are many things which we enjoy and find satisfying, even though we are not very good at performing them, even though we are not experts. Again, there are many things we are good at and even excel at but do not find very pleasing or satisfying.

Situation 23: I Always Procrastinate

Situation 23

A. *Activating Adverse Event*

There is a mountain of incomplete work. It's just my bad work habits, my perpetual procrastination. It's really making me anxious. I will never finish the work.

B. *Irrational Thought(s) I Have About A*

- I ALWAYS procrastinate (OVERGENERALIZATION).
- I will never finish it (EMOTIONAL REASONING, FORTUNE TELLING).
- The work load is enormous (BLACK-AND-WHITE THINKING).

C. *Consequences of Having Those Thoughts About A*

- Feeling inadequate
- Feeling hopeless

D. *Dispute the Irrational Thoughts in B*

- Where is the evidence that I ALWAYS procrastinate?
- How do I know that I will never finish the work?
- Why am I thinking that I will have to tackle the entire workload in one go?

E. *Effective New Thinking: Substitute Something Realistic and Rational Instead of B*

- I don't ALWAYS procrastinate. That statement is an overstatement, an exaggeration, and makes me feel as if procrastination is my inherent nature. That is definitely not correct. In fact, there are countless things that I do on time – for example, getting up in time to brush my teeth, having breakfast, doing my daily chores and going to the office. At the office, there have been many occasions when I have met deadlines successfully. I of course procrastinate about quite a few things, but definitely not everything.
- I may not desire to tackle the work; in fact, it's not necessary that I so desire. However, it would benefit me if I commence tackling the workload.

- I can prioritize and start with the tasks which are more urgent and important first. If I put off tackling the work, I will make myself more worried and agonized about the impending workload.
- I don't have to tackle all the tasks at one go. I can try to tackle piled up work in a phased manner by breaking it up in small time lots – say devoting 20 min per day to attacking piled up work. If I keep the figure small at say 20 min and know that I can quit after 20 min, it won't be too stressful – in fact, I will find it easier to get started and once started, I may feel like going on for longer than 20 min. The key here is to keep the goals modest, so that I feel more motivated to accomplish them. Once I know that I won't have to work for more than 20 min at a given time, the task will seem less overpowering and I won't be lured to put it off for later.
- Let me just start the work instead of waiting to get motivated. Let me plan to do say 10–15 min of work at the outset, on a daily basis. If I wait to get motivated, I may have to wait one more year. Always, motivation comes after the act of getting started. Once I start the work, motivation will definitely follow. I can give myself a reward once I get started on the job and maybe also reward myself for each phase of the job that I complete. The reward maybe anything I enjoy – for instance, eating a favourite food, reading something interesting, listening to good music or going somewhere nice.
- Piled up work is stressful and anxiety causing. From now onwards, what I can do is try to finish each piece of work immediately as and when it comes up, instead of letting it pile up. That way, I will not lose sleep over it.

Result: Not feeling as inadequate and feeling more motivated and encouraged to embark upon the task

Situation 24: I Am Always Indecisive

Situation 24

A. *Activating Adverse Event*

I have to take a decision on this matter soon. My head is reeling with options. I am so very indecisive that I cannot make up my mind. Now the tension is really becoming unbearable.

B. *Irrational Thought(s) I Have About A*

I am ALWAYS indecisive (OVERGENERALIZATION, LABELLING).

C. *Consequences of Having Those Beliefs About A*

- Feeling frustrated and confused
- Feeling incompetent

D. *Dispute the Irrational Thoughts in B*

- Is there any evidence that I am ALWAYS indecisive?

E. *Effective New Thoughts and Beliefs: Substitute Something Realistic and Rational Instead of B*

- I am not ALWAYS indecisive. That statement is a gross, fat exaggeration. Why is it an exaggeration? This is because I am always making decisions – today and every day. Today, for instance, I decided to come to office; then I decided to finish some tasks. Next, I decided to attend a meeting, and subsequently I decided to call up some of my customers and suppliers. After the phone calls were over, I decided to take a coffee break. In the late afternoon, I decided to go for a walk, followed by the decision to watch the evening news. At night after dinner, I decided to read a book. Afterwards, I decided to sleep. So I see that every single day I am making many decisions automatically – I am quite decisive as a matter of fact!
- Sure, in this particular case, because of the complexity of the issue, I am not being able to arrive at a decision quickly – this is perfectly natural. In fact, it might turn out to be good, since I am analysing all the options in detail. However, I must keep in mind that no decision I take will be the "perfect" decision, because there is no such a thing called perfect. Everything can be improved. What I can do in this case is to weigh the costs and benefits of each option and then decide to adopt the one where the benefits seem most favourable vis-à-vis the costs.
- I am overestimating the amount of responsibility and control that I have over whether the decision will ultimately turn out to be the best one. No one can foretell that. So many different variables can influence the operationalization of the decision and hence the outcome. I can only take what I think will be the best decision in terms of the pros and cons now.

Result: Feeling more confident about myself and more relaxed about taking the decision; no longer feeling inadequate

The Advantages of Cognitive Behavioural Therapy (CBT) in the Workplace

Cognitive behavioural techniques are one of the best approaches to helping employees cope with stress at the workplace and function more effectively at work. Let us revisit the statement we made in the beginning that in spite of all efforts made by the organization, employees never seem satisfied. What CBT recognizes is that changing A's when self-defeating B's are present is only dealing with the external symptoms and not analysing the underlying issues causing the problematic, unsettling behaviours. Organizations must be reoriented to understand that people do not always respond to a stimulus as you would like them to and that cognition is a significant factor in achieving and sustaining high morale. CBT can therefore be effectively used in the workplace in changing the self-defeating thoughts and behaviours that interfere with the achievement of personal and organizational goals and ensuring that employees do not react to adverse situations irrationally. CBT is the most user-friendly school of psychotherapy when it comes to helping companies solve people problems, enhance productivity and help employees become happier and more effective as workers, managers and leaders. Most importantly:

1. CBT is practical and results in effective real-time results. It is action-oriented. If we put in the effort, we can experience beneficial changes almost immediately.
2. CBT is simple yet immensely powerful. It is straightforward, objective and logical.
3. CBT focuses on the present rather than spending time, energy and money on searching the past for the origins of the present day issues.

Cognitive Behavioural Therapy (CBT) for Us

From the analyses of the various workplace stress scenarios above, we see that cognitive behavioural therapy (CBT) can be effectively used for a variety of situations which are troubling us in the workplace. Once we start questioning, challenging and disputing our irrational beliefs, we become less upset, less distressed and start focusing on solving our problems. Our entire outlook of life changes and we start pursuing a more cheerful, hopeful track.

The CBT approach makes us realize that all of us are defective in many ways – all of us have shortcomings, deficiencies and weaknesses. Nobody is perfect. This realistic, objective, unconditional and honest self-acceptance enables us to try to act upon and improve our shortcomings if we so desire and, most importantly, gives us a feeling of inner peace. It also reinforces the fact that we are always equal to other people – neither inferior nor superior to anyone else. Accomplishments, achievements and approvals do not constitute self-worth. We realize that we don't have to get what we want all the time to be adequate or worthwhile or valuable. This is because there is no definition of worth or value with regard to humanity. These are just notions and concepts. We are precious and worthy because we are humans. However, if we base our sense of self-worth and self-respect on our work or our accomplishments, then we will feel miserable in the absence of accomplishments, because there will be no other grounds for our satisfaction and self-esteem. This is one of the reasons that retired people (and even people who cannot continue to work because of accidents and sickness, or people whose businesses have collapsed, or whose careers have been ruined or stagnating for some reason) often feel useless, worthless and miserable. They get into the dysfunctional, distorted, inaccurate and unrealistic thinking pattern of equating accomplishments, productivity and success with happiness and self-worth. They forget that life offers a variety of opportunities (numerous hobbies, activities, interests, friends, family, the beauty of nature, social work – whatever makes us happy, the list is endless), outside of office work, that can also provide enjoyment and satisfaction. It is not required that one accomplishes a lot or experiences success in one's career in order to be happy and savour the richness of life. Most importantly, the happiness that we derive from our accomplishments is extremely fragile and fleeting. The day after our much sought after victory, we feel empty. On the contrary, we can feel happier if we can challenge our distorted, irrational and unrealistic thoughts and replace these with realistic, rational thoughts. A change in perspective is all that is needed. This alone leads to true mental empowerment.

It is amazing as to how much control we can exercise over our thought patterns – the liberation, the freedom and the breakthrough come when it is realized how much of our way of thinking is the result of conditioning and habit and how much this thinking leads to how we behave, without actually realizing that an alterable process is at work.

Chapter 6
Conclusion

So where does this leave us? We all have desires. Some of these desires may be:

- I want to achieve a lot and be very successful in my career.
- I want to be famous.
- I want to be wealthy.
- I want everybody to like me.
- I want everybody to behave well with me.
- I want to do meaningful, exciting work.

Desires and wants like these are absolutely normal. However, we invite trouble when we *take our desires, wants, goals, wishes and preferences and escalate them to DEMANDs* from ourselves and from others. We demand and insist that all our desires and preferences MUST, OUGHT, HAVE TO and SHOULD be fulfilled. We demand perfection from ourselves. We demand that we can never have any weaknesses, never act foolishly, never make mistakes, never act badly, never act selfishly and never act cruelly. Moreover, we fall into the trap of seeking perfectionism with regard to our emotional state. We feel distressed and ashamed of feelings such as anxiety, nervousness, boredom, depression, loneliness, panic, vulnerability and anger. We feel that we always ought to be cheerful, happy, confident, calm and in total control of our emotions. However, just like nothing or no situation can be perfect, just like we cannot achieve perfection in anything, similarly, we cannot always be peaceful and happy. It is not possible – our state of mind will change, just like a stream which is narrow at some points, wider at other points, lively and bubbling at some stretch, placid at another stretch, flat at certain points and twisting and meandering at other points. Our state of mind will change, because that is what is normal. If we can accept that sometimes we will feel nervous, anxious, vulnerable, bored, sad, jealous, scared, depressed, angry, demotivated, lonely and other negative emotions, then we are on the path to recovery and being cured. It is not possible to have "a perfect emotional or mental state" – perfectionism with regard to our mental condition or emotions is not attainable in reality. Neither is perfectionism with regard to our interpersonal relations. If we expect or desire that our close interactions with our friends, colleagues or anyone else will always be free of conflicts and

K. Choudhury, *Managing Workplace Stress: The Cognitive Behavioural Way*,
DOI 10.1007/978-81-322-0683-5_6, © Springer India 2013

other irritants, then our perfectionistic attitudes will only cause us sorrow, because they aim for impossible unattainable goals that will not be fulfilled in reality. This is because other people are just that - they are "others". They are different from us with different ways of thinking, different ideals, different desires, different self-interests and constraints, and hence will not often meet our expectations. For the same reason, even we will not meet their expectations always. Consequently, conflicts will arise.

With regard to adversities, the most common overstatements occur when we tell ourselves that we cannot stand or tolerate the situation. We convince ourselves that the situation is awful, terrible and horrible and say "I can't stand it". This is of course an exaggeration. What it means is "this situation will bring about my death". We may dislike certain situations intensely, but almost none of them are fatal. When we think that we can't stand or tolerate a situation, we reduce our ability to challenge it, address it and overcome it. We also tell ourselves that the situation MUST not exist. This kind of irrational thinking makes us become overwhelmed with our problems and feel hopeless. The fact is that the situation exists – hence, it MUST exist. We rarely can control the adversities that we confront. However, we do have control over how we think and feel about those adversities.

When something or someone goes against our desires, we have a choice of feeling healthy negative emotions such as feeling sorry or disappointed, OR we may choose to make ourselves depressed, miserable, terrified, panicked or insecure. Which emotions we choose depends on us. There is the option of choosing the rational set of thoughts and beliefs or what are called "preferences" in CBT. For instance, "I don't like what is going on; I wish it was not so. So let's see what I can do about it, if at all I can do anything about it. Otherwise, I will accept the fact that I cannot do anything about it and try to be content in spite of it". There is also the option of choosing irrational beliefs (in reaction to thwarted desires) or what are called "demands". For instance, "Because I don't like what is going on, it absolutely SHOULD not happen, it MUST not be, I CAN'T STAND IT, it's HORRIBLE and I think I'll give up."

Let us not forget that all the rules and demands we have represent absolutes held in our thinking that cannot be sustained or fulfilled in reality. Whenever we apply words like MUST, OUGHT or SHOULD to any situation or person, it is as if we are framing our own rules for life and the world to obey. However, life or the world does not work according to our rules; we see for ourselves that our rules are a mismatch with reality and what can be delivered by reality. This is why, when these rules, or our inner thinking and beliefs, are challenged and frustrated by reality, we become emotionally disturbed. So, let us use the techniques of CBT on the many situations that bother us in the workplace and elsewhere, in order to reclaim our peace of mind. Let us just start practising *looking for our DEMANDS and turning them into PREFERENCES.*

Thus, when an adverse event occurs, instead of telling ourselves that this condition MUST or SHOULD not occur, we accept it, though we may not like it. We accept it because this condition MUST occur since it has occurred. Acceptance is the key. When we accept it, (1) we recognize that the unpleasant event has happened and we don't insist or demand that it be otherwise or that it does not exist; (2) we don't exaggerate and regard it as terrible, horrible and awful; (3) we decide whether the situation can be improved; and (4) we do what we can to improve the situation or decide to be peaceful regardless of the situation (though we may not like it). We must remember that whenever we are horrified at adversities, it is because we are demanding that they do not exist.

With regard to achieving success, we feel that we need to be outstanding. This is our innate tendency as a human being and has been helpful in evolution. We feel the need to achieve more than others and show our superiority over them. Our culture also fosters this need for achievement and competitiveness, and no wonder it becomes very difficult to modify our ways of thinking. Difficult, of course, since it is tough to think and act rationally when irrationality is closing in on us from all sides. Difficult, yes, but not impossible.

CBT emphasizes the importance of what is called "unconditional self-acceptance." That is, we accept ourselves for what we are rather than for what we have achieved. Our self-respect and self-appreciation are grounded on a total acceptance of all our strengths, weaknesses and imperfections. All of us, each and every one of us has an intrinsic value as a human being, irrespective of what we have achieved, what accolades we have earned. Even if we have accomplished less than others, if we are less famous, less rich, less popular, less powerful, less influential or for that matter less anything, it just does not decrease our worth or value by even a speck; simply because, once again, there is no definition of human value or self-worth. To repeat, in the philosophy of CBT, each one of us is equal to the other – neither inferior nor superior. We realize that we don't NEED to be successful, and this change in outlook takes away the mad rush to outperform others, surpass them and show everybody that we are better than our competitors. This is because with the CBT philosophy we realize that even if we outshine and outperform others, this does not increase our intrinsic human value or worth and does not make us better than them. Similarly, when others surpass, outshine and outperform us, it does not make us less valuable, less important or less worthy. Our value, importance and worth as human beings are not in how we compare to others. This increases our sense of security and makes us pursue what we want to for ourselves and live life the way we want to. Moreover, when we understand that we don't need to succeed but would definitely like to, it takes off the pressure, the anxiety and the fear about failures (which can be debilitating), the fear of trying to go down untrodden paths. We accept the fact that we may do well sometimes, succeed sometimes, but not always, since perfection in achievements or anything else is not possible. This makes us work close to our full potential, concentrate on doing our job well and enjoy what we are doing, instead of worrying about unrealistic, perfectionistic achievement targets. It enables us to find fulfilment in our work instead of focusing only on whether we will achieve success. It enables us to focus on improving our own performance instead of worrying about outperforming others, becoming other-directed and then becoming depressed if we fail to outperform others. With the philosophy of CBT, we don't have to make the most of our full potential, not for ourselves, not for society. We only do so if it makes us happy and fulfilled. This enhances the quality of our work.

With regard to others, we think that the people concerned are our possessions, as if we own them. Hence, we demand that they behave exactly as we want them to do. CBT emphasizes that just as we accept ourselves unconditionally, we also accept others unconditionally. We realize that human beings are pretty complex, having many good and bad traits. While certain traits and behaviours may be undesirable, we cannot label an entire person to be "bad" based on them. Similarly, we cannot label an entire person as "good" based on certain traits and behaviours. Everyone behaves "well" and "badly" – they do good things and bad things. We accept that, just like we do, people will behave badly, incompetently, abominably, selfishly, immorally, cruelly and foolishly at times. We accept others with their failings and shortcomings, even though we may not like their "bad" behaviours. Of course, we can try to if possible avoid people whose behaviours we largely do not like. Moreover, we recognize that how a person behaves is dependent on his biological make-up, his genes, his culture, the way he has been raised and his life experiences. Unconditional acceptance of others thus decreases our unrealistic expectations that they will behave according to our wishes, values and expectations at all times. It decreases our anger, disturbances and sadness when others behave badly with us and when their attitudes don't live up to our expectations. We just prefer to have people behave well with us and feel healthily disappointed when they do not. Most importantly, we do not blame ourselves for the offensive behaviour of others since they are not under our control. Since they are not under our control, we realize that their behaviour is their responsibility, not ours. Likewise, we are not afraid of disagreements either, nor do we feel inferior, snubbed or insulted when others refuse to accept our advice or disobey us, since we cannot control others. We don't insist that others MUST agree with us, and because we don't try to control and dominate others, people find it pleasant to be in our company.

Last but not the least, the tendency of forming irrational, unrealistic, demanding, absolute, rigid, extreme and exaggerated views is universal. Everyone is doing it, since it's ingrained in our genes and nourished by our society, norms and culture. This implies that everybody is losing out on tranquillity and mental peace. The silver lining is that you don't have to lose. By being aware of your thought processes and disputing your cognitive errors and irrational thoughts time and again as outlined in this book, you will become increasingly effective at resolving the issues that cause you unhappiness. I hope this book will inspire you each and every day, whenever anything upsets you, to counteract your irrational thoughts with realistic, rational thoughts. The result? Feeling happier, increased serenity and peace of mind. After all, cognitive behavioural therapy is not just a therapeutic technique. It is a philosophy, a way of life.

Chapter 7
Exercises: Identifying and Challenging Distorted Negative Thoughts

Exercise 1: Lost Your Job

- You have received the termination notice (lay-off order) from your company. You breakdown and feel "This is so unfair. I failed as an employee. My life is over. I am a loser in every sense of the term".

  Write down at least six distortions in your way of thinking.

Distortions

Distortion 1:

Distortion 2:

Distortion 3:

K. Choudhury, *Managing Workplace Stress: The Cognitive Behavioural Way*,
DOI 10.1007/978-81-322-0683-5_7, © Springer India 2013

Distortion 4:

Distortion 5:

Distortion 6:

Write down your negative, upsetting thoughts. For each negative thought, counter it with a rational, realistic and positive thought.

Upsetting Thought	Rational, realistic and positive thought

Actions that I may take to deal with the situation:

Exercise 2: Failed in Your Job Interview

- You failed to get the job even though your interview went really well and your credentials were excellent. You later heard that the person selected is much less qualified and experienced than you are and much less appealing as a prospective employee in all ways. You tell yourself "Life is so unfair. This shouldn't have happened".

  Write down at least six distortions in your way of thinking.

Distortions

Distortion 1:

Distortion 2:

Distortion 3:

Distortion 4:

Distortion 5:

Distortion 6:

Write down your negative, upsetting thoughts. For each negative thought, counter it with a rational, realistic and positive thought.

Upsetting Thought	Rational, realistic and positive thought

Actions that I may take to deal with the situation:

Exercise 3: Not the All-Rounder

- You are kind of new at the office, and your office colleagues have organized a cricket match. You have been asked to be in the team. In fact, your boss who is always talking of tea m spirit has specifically conveyed that you must join the team and the game. You know that you are not at all a good player, and this is making you extremely anxious. You are cringing at the thought of making a fool of yourself, what with the general belief that goes around, about men being the sport-loving types.

  Write down at least six distortions in your way of thinking.

Distortions

Distortion 1:

Distortion 2:

Distortion 3:

Distortion 4:

Distortion 5:

Distortion 6:

Write down your negative, upsetting thoughts. For each negative thought, counter it with a rational, realistic and positive thought.

Upsetting Thought	Rational, realistic and positive thought

Actions that I may take to deal with the situation:

Exercise 4: Feeling Inferior

- You failed to get the promotion that you think you highly deserved and which you were anxiously waiting for. You think "I am inferior to my colleagues, since no one so far has ever failed to get a promotion in this office. Everyone will think badly about me".

  Write down at least six distortions in your way of thinking.

Distortions

Distortion 1:

Distortion 2:

Distortion 3:

Distortion 4:

Distortion 5:

Distortion 6:

Write down your negative, upsetting thoughts. For each negative thought, counter it with a rational, realistic and positive thought.

Upsetting Thought	Rational, realistic and positive thought

Actions that I may take to deal with the situation:

Exercise 5: Mundane Work

- Your job in the office pays well but is mundane. You are bored and fed up and feel "I MUST not be doing routine work".

  Write down at least six distortions in your way of thinking.

Distortions

Distortion 1:

Distortion 2:

Distortion 3:

Distortion 4:

Distortion 5:

Distortion 6:

Write down your negative, upsetting thoughts. For each negative thought, counter it with a rational, realistic and positive thought.

Upsetting Thought	Rational, realistic and positive thought

Actions that I may take to deal with the situation:

Exercise 6: Being Laughed At

- You saw some colleagues laughing when you were giving a talk (speech). You think, "This means that my speech was bad, a waste of time, and they found me comic as a person. They must have thought that my speech had no substance and so they were absorbed in their own jokes".

  Write down at least six distortions in your way of thinking.

Distortions

Distortion 1:

Distortion 2:

Distortion 3:

Distortion 4:

Distortion 5:

Distortion 6:

Write down your negative, upsetting thoughts. For each negative thought, counter it with a rational, realistic and positive thought.

Upsetting Thought	Rational, realistic and positive thought

Actions that I may take to deal with the situation:

Exercise 7: The Boss Is Dumping His Work on You

- You have a huge workload and it is a particularly busy day. Your boss suddenly dumps some of his own work on you, saying that he has to make a visit to the doctor. You know that he often goes for routine medical checks. You are frustrated and tell yourself "This is grossly unfair. Why can he not pick on others?"

  Write down at least six distortions in your way of thinking.

Distortions

Distortion 1:

Distortion 2:

Distortion 3:

Distortion 4:

Distortion 5:

Distortion 6:

Write down your negative, upsetting thoughts. For each negative thought, counter it with a rational, realistic and positive thought.

Upsetting Thought	Rational, realistic and positive thought

Actions that I may take to deal with the situation:

Exercise 8: Feel Incompetent

- Your superior has asked you to do the feasibility study for a project. You know that you are not particularly good at this sort of thing, especially work involving number crunching. You tell yourself, "If I cannot do a piece of work perfectly, I won't do it at all. I will go and tell my superior that I am no good at this".

  Write down at least six distortions in your way of thinking.

Distortions

Distortion 1:

Distortion 2:

Distortion 3:

Distortion 4:

Distortion 5:

Distortion 6:

Write down your negative, upsetting thoughts. For each negative thought, counter it with a rational, realistic and positive thought.

Upsetting Thought	Rational, realistic and positive thought

Actions that I may take to deal with the situation:

Exercise 9: Can't Stand Up for Yourself

- Your colleague has wrongly accused you of compromising your integrity with respect to a particular sales transaction and has reported you to the boss. The boss has called you to his office in an hour's time. You feel from your past experience that you will not be able to stand up for yourself and assertively communicate your views. You feel extremely apprehensive and scared.

  Write down at least six distortions in your way of thinking.

Distortions

Distortion 1:

Distortion 2:

Distortion 3:

Distortion 4:

Distortion 5:

Distortion 6:

Write down your negative, upsetting thoughts. For each negative thought, counter it with a rational, realistic and positive thought.

Upsetting Thought	Rational, realistic and positive thought

Actions that I may take to deal with the situation:

Exercise 10: Boss Does Not Like You

- Your irritable, cantankerous boss often snaps at you. Today, he angrily shouted at you. You think that "The boss does not like me. If he did, he would not behave with me like that".

  Write down at least six distortions in your way of thinking.

Distortions

Distortion 1:

Distortion 2:

Distortion 3:

Distortion 4:

Distortion 5:

Distortion 6:

Write down your negative, upsetting thoughts. For each negative thought, counter it with a rational, realistic and positive thought.

Upsetting Thought	Rational, realistic and positive thought

Actions that I may take to deal with the situation:

Exercise 11: Failed to Do What You Had Planned

- You are very disappointed. You had made a methodical list of all the very important and urgent jobs that you were to complete today in office. However, you could not complete some of them. You feel dejected.

  Write down at least six distortions in your way of thinking.

Distortions

Distortion 1:

Distortion 2:

Distortion 3:

Distortion 4:

Distortion 5:

Distortion 6:

Write down your negative, upsetting thoughts. For each negative thought, counter it with a rational, realistic and positive thought.

Upsetting Thought	Rational, realistic and positive thought

Actions that I may take to deal with the situation:

Exercise 12: Lack Common Sense

- When you approached your boss with the news about a crucial project which you had completed quite successfully, he snapped at you saying, "For heaven's sake don't disturb me now! Don't barge in like that". You feel downright humiliated and ashamed and tell yourself "When will I ever develop some sense and sophistication? When will I learn what is and what is not appropriate? I am a total oaf, a clumsy lout, an out and out fool".

  Write down at least six distortions in your way of thinking.

Distortions

Distortion 1:

Distortion 2:

Distortion 3:

Distortion 4:

Distortion 5:

Distortion 6:

Write down your negative, upsetting thoughts. For each negative thought, counter it with a rational, realistic and positive thought.

Upsetting Thought	Rational, realistic and positive thought

Actions that I may take to deal with the situation:

Exercise 13: You Help Others but They Don't Help You

- You have always helped your colleague whenever he has sought your help. However, once or twice when you asked him to help you, he has been evasive or given excuses … in short, he has not helped you. You are quite taken aback and find this situation unfair and painful, since you have always helped him whenever he has asked you.

  Write down at least six distortions in your way of thinking.

Distortions

Distortion 1:

Distortion 2:

Distortion 3:

Distortion 4:

Distortion 5:

Distortion 6:

Write down your negative, upsetting thoughts. For each negative thought, counter it with a rational, realistic and positive thought.

Upsetting Thought	Rational, realistic and positive thought

Actions that I may take to deal with the situation:

Exercise 14: Feeling Inferior

- Your colleague, who is about the same age as you are, is achieving much more than you in terms of office performance. His performance is way superior to yours. You are of course quite talented in certain other areas like tennis and playing the drums. However, even your colleague is very good (as good as you are) when it comes to these hobbies. You feel inferior and inadequate, since he happens to be much better than you in the very important area of workplace performance and just as good as you in hobbies as well. You think that there should be at least one activity where you should excel at and be better than him.

  Write down at least six distortions in your way of thinking.

Distortions

Distortion 1:

Distortion 2:

Distortion 3:

Distortion 4:

Distortion 5:

Distortion 6:

Write down your negative, upsetting thoughts. For each negative thought, counter it with a rational, realistic and positive thought.

Upsetting Thought	Rational, realistic and positive thought

Actions that I may take to deal with the situation:

Exercise 15: Never Speak Up at Meetings

- You usually never speak up in office meetings, especially the big ones. You fear that you might say something wrong.

  Write down at least six distortions in your way of thinking.

Distortions

Distortion 1:

Distortion 2:

Distortion 3:

Distortion 4:

Distortion 5:

Distortion 6:

Write down your negative, upsetting thoughts. For each negative thought, counter it with a rational, realistic and positive thought.

Upsetting Thought	Rational, realistic and positive thought

Actions that I may take to deal with the situation:

Exercise 16: Never Speak Up at Meetings (This Time for a Different Reason)

- You usually never speak up in office meetings, especially the big ones. You fear that you might say something foolish.

  Write down at least six distortions in your way of thinking.

Distortions

Distortion 1:

Distortion 2:

Distortion 3:

Distortion 4:

Distortion 5:

Distortion 6:

Write down your negative, upsetting thoughts. For each negative thought, counter it with a rational, realistic and positive thought.

Upsetting Thought	Rational, realistic and positive thought

Actions that I may take to deal with the situation:

Exercise 17: Never Speak Up at Meetings (For Yet Another Reason)

- You usually never speak up in office meetings, especially the big ones. You fear that you might say something that others may not agree with.

  Write down at least six distortions in your way of thinking.

Distortions

Distortion 1:

Distortion 2:

Distortion 3:

Distortion 4:

Distortion 5:

Distortion 6:

Write down your negative, upsetting thoughts. For each negative thought, counter it with a rational, realistic and positive thought.

Upsetting Thought	Rational, realistic and positive thought

Actions that I may take to deal with the situation:

Exercise 18: Complaint Against You

- One of your customers (and he is a big customer) has complained about you to your boss, saying that you were rude and incompetent. You feel “My boss will think that I am a bad salesperson”.

  Write down at least six distortions in your way of thinking.

Distortions

Distortion 1:

Distortion 2:

Distortion 3:

Distortion 4:

Distortion 5:

Distortion 6:

Write down your negative, upsetting thoughts. For each negative thought, counter it with a rational, realistic and positive thought.

Upsetting Thought	Rational, realistic and positive thought

Actions that I may take to deal with the situation:

Exercise 19: Impress the Chairman

- The chairman of your board is coming to your office today and has conveyed that he would like to meet a few selected managers individually. You are among the selected few. You are nervous and uptight, thinking "I am not at all good in small talk. Neither am I very smooth and fluent. What if I am suddenly at a loss of things to say in mid-conversation? He will think what an unimpressive, unintelligent, uncool guy I am".

Write down at least six distortions in your way of thinking.

Distortions

Distortion 1:

Distortion 2:

Distortion 3:

Distortion 4:

Distortion 5:

Distortion 6:

Write down your negative, upsetting thoughts. For each negative thought, counter it with a rational, realistic and positive thought.

Upsetting Thought	Rational, realistic and positive thought

Actions that I may take to deal with the situation:

Exercise 20: A Disastrous Day

- In the morning, you had a heated argument with one of your suppliers. In the afternoon, you came to know that the customer whom you had been wining and dining for quite some time has placed a big order with your competitor instead. You feel "My day was a total disaster".

  Write down at least six distortions in your way of thinking.

Distortions

Distortion 1:

Distortion 2:

Distortion 3:

Distortion 4:

Distortion 5:

Distortion 6:

Write down your negative, upsetting thoughts. For each negative thought, counter it with a rational, realistic and positive thought.

Upsetting Thought	Rational, realistic and positive thought

Actions that I may take to deal with the situation:

Exercise 21: Interview After-Effects

- You have given an interview. It didn't go as well as you would have liked. You are dismayed with yourself, saying over and over "How could I answer those two questions incorrectly? I knew the answers. Why didn't I take some time and think about them instead of blurting out the wrong answers? This is unforgiveable".

  Write down at least six distortions in your way of thinking.

Distortions

Distortion 1:

Distortion 2:

Distortion 3:

Distortion 4:

Distortion 5:

Distortion 6:

Write down your negative, upsetting thoughts. For each negative thought, counter it with a rational, realistic and positive thought.

Upsetting Thought	Rational, realistic and positive thought

Actions that I may take to deal with the situation:

Exercise 22: Anxiety Jitters at Presentations

- You have been asked to give a presentation to a gathering of senior executives in the company. Your heart is beating really fast and your palms are already sweaty. You feel jumpy, anxious and nervous and think "My presentation will not be smooth and flawless like some other people's are. I just don't have the style. I will miss out on the important points. I will probably stutter and forget what I have to say somewhere into the presentation. I will look like an incompetent, nervous fool".

  Write down at least six distortions in your way of thinking.

Distortions

Distortion 1:

Distortion 2:

Distortion 3:

Distortion 4:

Distortion 5:

Distortion 6:

Write down your negative, upsetting thoughts. For each negative thought, counter it with a rational, realistic and positive thought.

Upsetting Thought	Rational, realistic and positive thought

Actions that I may take to deal with the situation:

Exercise 23: Not Popular

- A bunch of your colleagues were chatting near the coffee machine. Even though you stood there, they did not acknowledge your presence and carried on with their conversation. You think "They do not like me or do not like me enough".

  Write down at least six distortions in your way of thinking.

Distortions

Distortion 1:

Distortion 2:

Distortion 3:

Distortion 4:

Distortion 5:

Distortion 6:

Write down your negative, upsetting thoughts. For each negative thought, counter it with a rational, realistic and positive thought.

Upsetting Thought	Rational, realistic and positive thought

Actions that I may take to deal with the situation:

Exercise 24: Ethical Dilemma

- You are in the Marketing Division of a company. You have done a market survey of your customers and have found that your company's salespeople have severe attitudinal and performance problems that customers are very dissatisfied with. You have to submit a written report on the results of your survey to the Vice-Presidents, the President and the Chief Executive Officer of your company. The Chief Sales Officer however has requested you to delete the customers' disparaging comments from the report (which would be widely circulated), saying that the very fact that you have verbally conveyed the unhappy customers' comments to the Sales Division is good enough and that they would act on it. You feel pressured and bewildered thinking "This is so unfair. I should not be asked to do such things. I should be able to work independently, with integrity and according to my ideals and principles. If I yield to these pressures, I will be doing injustice to my company".

  Write down at least six distortions in your way of thinking.

Distortions

Distortion 1:

Distortion 2:

Distortion 3:

Distortion 4:

Distortion 5:

Distortion 6:

Write down your negative, upsetting thoughts. For each negative thought, counter it with a rational, realistic and positive thought.

Upsetting Thought	Rational, realistic and positive thought

Actions that I may take to deal with the situation:

References

Beck AT (1976) Cognitive therapy and the emotional disorders. International Universities Press, New York
Beck AT, Emery G, Greenberg R (2005) Anxiety disorders and phobias: a cognitive perspective. Basic Books, New York
Burns D (1999) Feeling good: the new mood therapy, Harper. Harper Paperback Print, 2009
Ellis A (2001) Feeling better, getting better, staying better: profound self-help therapy for your emotions. Impact Publishers Inc., Atascadero (Second Printing, January 2002)
Ellis A (2007) How to make yourself happy and remarkably less disturbable. Impact Publishers Inc., Atascadero (Seventh Printing, May 2008)
Ellis A, Harper RA (1997) A guide to rational living. Melvin Powers Wilshire Book Company, Chatsworth

K. Choudhury, *Managing Workplace Stress: The Cognitive Behavioural Way*,
DOI 10.1007/978-81-322-0683-5, © Springer India 2013

About the Author

Dr. Koushiki Choudhury teaches at the Indian Institute of Management Calcutta. She has completed her Master's degree from the Pennsylvania State University, USA and her doctorate from the Indian Institute of Management Calcutta. She was a visiting scholar at the University of California, USA and the Curtin University, Australia. Dr. Choudhury's educational, research, teaching and consultancy interests include internal marketing and its interface with the behavioural sciences and human resources, psychological counselling and relationship marketing. She has had extensive experience in these areas in the corporate sector, where she worked for several years before joining academics.

K. Choudhury, *Managing Workplace Stress: The Cognitive Behavioural Way*,
DOI 10.1007/978-81-322-0683-5, © Springer India 2013

Index

A
ABC Framework, 13–17
Adverse, 8, 13–16, 19, 20, 26, 37, 39, 41–43, 45, 46, 48–50, 52, 54–58, 60, 61, 63, 64, 66–70, 72, 76
Adversity, 52, 76, 77
All-or-nothing thinking, 20
Anxiety, 1, 4, 7–9, 13, 15, 19, 20, 25–28, 32, 33, 35, 70, 75, 77, 106–107
Assumptions, 19, 22, 23, 46, 68
AWFUL, 9, 11, 35

B
Beck, A.T., 19, 20, 25, 26
Black and white thinking, 20, 38, 41, 48, 51, 64, 69
Burns, D., 20, 27

C
Catastrophization/catastrophizing, 22, 45–49, 58, 62–64
Cognitive behavioural therapy (CBT), 5, 35, 37–73, 76–78
Cognitive distortions, 24
Cognitive errors, 20–22, 25, 26, 35, 37, 52, 78
Cognitive therapy (CT), 5, 19–35

D
Demanding, 8, 9, 17, 23, 35, 62, 77, 78
Demands, 1, 4, 8–10, 24, 25, 35, 43, 50, 56, 59, 75–78
Dichotomous thinking, 20
Dispute, 8, 9, 13, 34, 38, 40, 41, 43–45, 47–49, 51, 53, 54, 56–58, 60, 62, 63, 65–69, 71
Disputing, 11–12, 16–17, 72, 78
Disqualifying the positive bias, 22
Downward Arrow Technique, 27, 28, 32
Dysfunctional beliefs, 25–34, 50

E
Ellis, A., 7
Emotional reasoning, 21, 44, 46, 51, 52, 55, 58, 68, 69

F
Fortune-telling, 21, 41, 52, 55, 69

H
Harper, R.A., 7–9, 13, 22
HAVE TOs, 9, 10, 33, 35, 49, 51, 52, 54, 55, 63, 66, 75
High frustration tolerance, 11
HORRIBLE, 9, 11, 35, 76
Human value, 41, 54, 56, 77
Human worth, 26, 38–40, 45, 54, 56, 59, 66

I
Irrational beliefs, 7–13, 34, 35, 72, 76
Irrational core beliefs, 8–9
Irrational thinking, 8, 12, 76
Irrational thoughts, 8, 12, 13, 38, 40–49, 51–58, 60, 62–71, 78

K. Choudhury, *Managing Workplace Stress: The Cognitive Behavioural Way*,
DOI 10.1007/978-81-322-0683-5, © Springer India 2013

L
Labelling, 21, 32, 38, 41, 42, 44, 48, 51, 53, 58, 64, 70
Low-frustration tolerance, 8, 9

M
Magnification, 38, 41, 63, 68
Mental filter, 38, 41, 48, 51, 63, 64
Mind-reading, 21, 41, 44, 53
Minimization, 22
MUST, 8–12, 15, 16, 21, 33, 35, 38, 40, 42, 44, 47, 49, 51, 54–60, 63–66, 75, 76, 78, 84

N
NATs. *See* Negative automatic thoughts (NATs)
NEED, 9, 16, 44, 55, 56, 66, 77
Negative automatic thoughts (NATs), 25–31

O
OUGHTS, 9, 35, 51, 75, 76
Overgeneralization, 20, 49, 55, 63, 69, 70

P
Perfect, 10, 25, 27, 32, 38–41, 43, 51, 59, 64, 67, 68, 71, 72, 75
Perfection, 39, 43, 56, 75, 77
Perfectionism, 20, 60, 75
Perfectionistic, 24, 43, 52, 56, 60, 66, 76, 77
Personalization, 21–22, 44, 64
Positive, 1, 8, 11, 20, 22, 25, 43, 55, 64, 80, 81, 83–94, 96–107, 109, 110

R
Rational beliefs, 11, 13
Rational emotive behaviour therapy (REBT), 5, 7–9, 11–17, 34–35
Rational responses, 24, 28–32
Rational thinking, 7, 8
Rational thoughts, 7, 20, 73, 78
Realistic, 9, 11, 19, 20, 23, 26, 28, 32, 34, 38–73, 78, 80, 81, 83–94, 96–107, 109, 110
REBT. *See* Rational emotive behaviour therapy (REBT)

S
Selective abstraction, 20
SHOULDs, 9–12, 16, 23, 35, 40, 42, 45–47, 49–51, 57–59, 62, 63, 67, 68, 75, 76

T
TERRIBLE, 9, 11, 35, 64

U
Unconditional life-acceptance, 9, 11
Unconditional other-acceptance, 9, 10
Unconditional self-acceptance, 9–11, 77
Unrealistic, 2, 8, 9, 12, 20, 23, 24, 26, 28, 32, 33, 35, 38, 40, 43, 51, 52, 59, 64, 66, 73, 77, 78

V
Values, 3, 10, 23, 24, 30–32, 38–45, 47, 54, 56, 59, 65, 66, 72, 77, 78

W
Workplace, 1–5, 9, 17, 21, 23, 37–73, 76, 96

MIX
Papier aus verantwortungsvollen Quellen
Paper from responsible sources
FSC® C105338

If you have any concerns about our products,
you can contact us on
ProductSafety@springernature.com

In case Publisher is established outside the EU,
the EU authorized representative is:
Springer Nature Customer Service Center GmbH
Europaplatz 3, 69115 Heidelberg, Germany

Printed by Libri Plureos GmbH
in Hamburg, Germany